September 6, 2013

The Honorable Bernard Sanders
Chairman
Subcommittee on Primary Health and Aging
Committee on Health, Education, Labor, and Pensions
United States Senate

Dear Mr. Chairman:

More than a decade ago, the Surgeon General's report on oral health described the poor oral health of our nation as a "silent epidemic."[1] Today, high rates of dental diseases remain prevalent across the nation, especially in vulnerable and underserved populations. The cost of dental care and lack of dental coverage are often cited as reasons individuals may not seek needed dental care.[2] In 2008, 42 percent of adults with tooth or mouth problems reported they did not see a dentist because they did not have dental coverage or could not afford the out-of-pocket payments.[3] Similarly, in 2011, 4 million children did not obtain needed dental care because their families could not afford it.[4] The Institute of Medicine has reported that there is strong evidence that dental coverage is positively associated with access to and use of oral health care.[5]

---

[1] U.S. Department of Health and Human Services, National Institute of Dental and Craniofacial Research, National Institutes of Health, *Oral Health in America: A Report of the Surgeon General* (Rockville, Md.: 2000).

[2] Individuals can obtain dental coverage from private insurance or public programs including Medicaid, Medicare, Veterans Affairs, or state sponsored programs.

[3] B. Bloom, C.M. Simile, P.F. Adams, and R.A. Cohen, *Oral Health Status and Access to Oral Health Care for U.S. Adults Aged 18–64: National Health Interview Survey 2008*, Vital and Health Statistics 10(253) (Hyattsville, Md.: National Center for Health Statistics, 2012). For our report, insurance premiums were not included in out-of-pocket payments.

[4] B. Bloom, R.A. Cohen, and G. Freeman, *Summary Health Statistics for U.S. Children: National Health Interview Survey, 2011*, Vital and Health Statistics 10(254) (Hyattsville, Md.: National Center for Health Statistics, 2012).

[5] Institute of Medicine and National Research Council, *Improving Access to Oral Health Care for Vulnerable and Underserved Populations*. The National Academies Press (Washington, D.C.: 2011). For example, one study found that individuals who did not have dental insurance were about two-thirds less likely to have a dental visit than individuals with private insurance.

Recognizing that oral health is central to a person's overall health and well-being, the Department of Health and Human Services (HHS) has adopted an oral health objective as a leading health indicator in its Healthy People 2020 initiative, which consists of 10-year national objectives for improving the health of all Americans.[6] Specifically, HHS's leading indicator for oral health is to increase the proportion of children, adolescents, and adults who used the oral health care system in the past 12 months. The 2020 target for this leading health indicator is to increase access to dental services—increasing the proportion of individuals aged 2 years and older who have had a dental visit in a year to 49.0 percent from 44.5 percent in 2007.

Many families that cannot afford dental care obtain it from health centers, for which federal funds provide a substantial part of revenue. Dental services that are provided by health centers must be available to all patients, regardless of their ability to pay. All health centers must have fee schedules for all services, including any dental services provided, that reflect prevailing fees in the area and a schedule of discounts (or sliding fee schedule) for individuals who earn annual incomes equal to or less than 200 percent of the federal poverty level (FPL).

You asked us to examine dental coverage, and use of and payments for dental services in the United States. This report describes (1) trends in coverage for and use of dental services, (2) trends in payments for dental services made by individuals and other payers, and (3) the extent to which dental fees vary between and within selected communities across the nation. You also asked us to examine national expenditures for dental services. We report national dental expenditures from 1996 through 2011 in appendix I.

To provide information on trends in dental coverage and the use of dental services by type of coverage, we obtained and analyzed data files from the Medical Expenditure Panel Survey (MEPS) for 1996, 2004, and 2010 on dental visits, dental services, and coverage status. We selected these

---

[6]Healthy People 2020 is an HHS initiative that provides science-based, 10-year national objectives for improving the health of all Americans. Healthy People establishes benchmarks and monitors progress over time in order to encourage collaborations across communities and sectors, empower individuals toward making informed health decisions, and measure the impact of prevention activities. See http://www.healthypeople.gov/about/default.aspx for more information.

years for our analysis because 1996 was the first year MEPS was administered and 2010 was the most recent year for which data were available; we included 2004 to provide three points in time for our analysis. MEPS is administered by HHS's Agency for Healthcare Research and Quality (AHRQ) and is a nationally representative survey of the noninstitutionalized population, including families, medical providers, and employers across the United States. We based our analysis on a similar analysis conducted by AHRQ for its Chartbook 17 publication.[7] We analyzed data on dental coverage and dental visits (including the category of service obtained during the visit, such as preventive or restorative) per year, as well as differences in coverage status and dental visits based on demographics such as age group and income level. We also examined use of dental services by individuals in urban and rural areas; to ensure adequate sample sizes, we combined several years of MEPS data. Information for the urban and rural analysis is presented in appendix II. MEPS collects information on private dental coverage but does not collect information specifically about whether dental coverage is included in health plans offered by public programs such as health coverage provided by the Department of Veterans Affairs (VA), Department of Defense (DOD), or Medicare Advantage.[8] Therefore, we could not determine for this population whether those individuals had dental coverage, and we categorized that group as unknown.

To identify trends in dental payments by individuals and other payers, that is, how much individuals paid out of pocket for dental care and how much dental insurers or other payers, such as Medicaid, paid for dental claims, we obtained and analyzed MEPS 1996, 2004, and 2010 data files on

---

[7]Chartbook 17 examined MEPS data related to dental coverage, use, and payments in 1996 and 2004. R.J. Manski and E. Brown, *Dental Use, Expenses, Private Dental Coverage, and Changes, 1996 and 2004*, MEPS Chartbook No.17 (Rockville, Md.: Agency for Healthcare Research and Quality, 2007). See http://www.meps.ahrq.gov/mepsweb/data_files/publications/cb17/cb17.pdf.

[8]Medicare Part A covers hospital and other inpatient stays. Medicare Part B is optional insurance and covers hospital outpatient, physician, and other services. Medicare beneficiaries have the option of obtaining coverage for Medicare Part A and B services from private health plans that participate in the Medicare Advantage program—also known as Medicare Part C. Medicare Advantage is a private plan alternative to traditional Medicare fee-for-service and may provide benefits, such as dental coverage, not included in traditional Medicare fee-for-service. In 2010, about 25 percent of Medicare beneficiaries were enrolled in Medicare Advantage plans.

dental visits, payments, and coverage status.[9] In addition, we analyzed variances by demographic group, including age group and income level.

To determine the extent to which dental fees varied between and within certain communities, we analyzed dental claims data compiled by FAIR Health, Inc. as of January 2013,[10] and obtained dental fee schedules from selected federally funded health centers. The FAIR Health dental data set contains over 140 million claims, including geozip data (the first 3 digits of a postal zip code[11]) and American Dental Association (ADA) Current Dental Terminology (CDT) billing codes.[12] We selected 24 dental procedures for comparison by identifying the CDT billing codes with the most dental claims in each of six categories of dental services—five codes each for diagnostic, preventive, and restorative services; and three each for endodontic, periodontic, and oral surgery services. Academic experts and ADA officials agreed that our list of 24 CDT codes was representative of the most common dental procedures. To select large communities, we identified the geozip with the most dental claims in the core city in the largest metropolitan statistical area in each of the nine U.S. Census Bureau divisions.[13] For comparison to our large communities, we selected nine small communities in the same states based on their population. Because geozip boundaries do not align with

---

[9]For this report, we refer to MEPS dental expenses as dental payments.

[10]FAIR Health, Inc., is an independent, not-for-profit corporation that compiles dental and medical claims data (nondiscounted fees charged by providers) from private insurers. See http://www.fairhealth.org/ for more information about FAIR Health, Inc., and its dental claims data set.

[11]FAIR Health uses the term geozip to refer to an area covered by the first 3 digits of a postal zip code. The U.S. Postal Service describes a 3-digit zip code as the area served by a sectional center facility, which is a processing and distribution center for all zip codes beginning with those 3 digits. Larger cities can include multiple 3-digit zip codes. For example, the Los Angeles/Long Beach metropolitan area includes geozips 900 to 912 (excluding 909).

[12]Codes on Dental Procedure and Nomenclature are the intellectual property of the ADA as copyright owner.

[13]The U.S. Office of Management and Budget delineates metropolitan statistical areas according to published standards that are applied to Census Bureau data. The general concept of a metropolitan statistical area is that of a core area containing a substantial population nucleus, together with adjacent communities having a high degree of economic and social integration with that core. The Census Bureau has nine divisions: New England, Middle Atlantic, East North Central, West North Central, South Atlantic, East South Central, West South Central, Mountain, and Pacific.

metropolitan statistical area designations, we selected one geozip (the one with the most dental claims) to represent each large and each small metropolitan area. We examined the 50th percentile dental fee and the 95th percentile dental fee for each of our 24 CDT codes from a geozip in each large and small community.[14] To identify dental fees charged by federally funded health centers, we obtained documentation and met with officials from HHS's Health Resources and Services Administration (HRSA), which administers the Health Center Program. HRSA provided a list of health centers that served residents of our 18 selected communities and that provided dental services. We obtained full fee and sliding fee schedules from one health center that served each community, although some health centers did not provide or bill separately for all 24 procedures.

To determine the reliability of the MEPS, FAIR Health, and health center data, we reviewed related documentation, talked to agency officials and academic experts, and reviewed other studies that used the data to address similar research questions. We determined that the MEPS, FAIR Health, and health center data were sufficiently reliable for the purposes of our report.

We conducted this performance audit from October 2012 to September 2013 in accordance with generally accepted government auditing standards. Those standards require that we plan and perform the audit to obtain sufficient, appropriate evidence to provide a reasonable basis for our findings and conclusions based on our audit objectives. We believe that the evidence obtained provides a reasonable basis for our findings and conclusions based on our audit objectives. (For more information on our scope and methodology, see app. III.)

---

[14]Percentiles indicate the percentage of reported fees that are below the stated amount; for example, 95 percent of reported fees fall below the 95th percentile.

Background

Dental Services

Dental services cover an array of procedures, from preventive services, such as cleanings, to more complex services, such as root canals (see table 1).

Table 1: Categories and Examples of Dental Services

Category	Examples
Diagnostic	• X-ray • Examination
Preventive	• Cleaning • Fluoride application • Sealant application
Restorative	• Fillings • Crowns
Endodontic	• Root canal
Periodontic	• Treatment of the gums
Oral Surgery	• Surgical removal of a tooth

Source: GAO summary of American Dental Association (ADA) information.

Dental Coverage

Most individuals with dental coverage have private dental insurance. Private dental insurance plans may be a stand-alone plan or be included as a part of medical insurance. Stand-alone dental plans require individuals to enroll separately; they are not a part of the individual's medical insurance plan. The types of dental services covered by dental plans vary widely among private plans. For example, one plan may include "comprehensive" care such as routine diagnostic and preventive services, restorative services, and oral surgery, while another may cover more limited services such as emergency care only. Cost sharing for dental services usually involves an annual deductible—and according to a Bureau of Labor Statistics survey of employers, in 2008, the median deductible was $50 per person.[15] After the individual meets the

---

[15]Bureau of Labor Statistics, *Selected Medical Benefits: A Report from the Department of Labor to the Department of Health and Human Services* (Washington, D.C.: Apr. 15, 2011). This survey was conducted by the Bureau of Labor Statistics of employer-sponsored health plans to determine the benefits typically covered by employers.

deductible, dental plans may pay a percentage of covered services up to a maximum annual benefit. In 2008, the reported median annual maximum was $1,500.

Individuals may also obtain dental coverage in other ways, such as through federal programs. Federal programs may cover dental services as a required benefit, support purchase of stand-alone dental coverage for eligible beneficiaries, or support coverage of dental services as part of broader coverage under individuals' medical coverage plans, for example. Benefits included in these types of coverage may vary widely depending on factors such as type of plan purchased, family income, or veteran's status (see table 2).

Table 2: Descriptions of Dental Coverage within Certain Federal Health Programs

Program	Description of dental coverage
Medicaid[a] and State Children's Health Insurance Program (CHIP)	For children in Medicaid, under the Early and Periodic Screening, Diagnostic, and Treatment benefit, state Medicaid programs must provide dental services, including diagnostic, preventive, and related treatment services, for all eligible Medicaid beneficiaries under age 21. For adults in Medicaid, dental coverage varies, as states have flexibility to determine whether to provide dental benefits for adults and if so, what services to include. For example, while many states cover some dental services for adults, such as preventive exams, other states do not, limiting this benefit to trauma care or emergency treatment for pain relief and infection. States may also require that certain services have prior approval, or place limits on the total amount of services an enrollee can receive each year.
	When CHIP was established in 1997, coverage of dental services was not a required benefit.[b] The Children's Health Insurance Program Reauthorization Act of 2009 expanded federal requirements for CHIP programs to cover dental services.[c] Specifically, the act required states to cover dental services in their CHIP programs beginning in October 2009. It also gave states authority to use benchmark plans to define the benefit package or to supplement children's private health insurance with a dental coverage plan financed through CHIP. States that provide CHIP coverage to children through a Medicaid expansion program are required to provide the Early and Periodic Screening, Diagnostic, and Treatment benefit. States with a separate CHIP program may choose from two options for providing dental coverage: a package of dental benefits that meets the CHIP requirements, or a benchmark dental benefit package that is substantially equal to the (1) most popular federal employee dental plan for dependents, (2) most popular plan selected for dependents in the state's employee dental plan, or (3) dental coverage offered through the most popular commercial insurer in the state.
Medicare	Generally, Medicare does not cover routine preventive or restorative dental services. Medicare fee-for-service offers dental coverage under limited circumstances, for example, providing dental services that are an integral part of a covered procedure (e.g., reconstruction of the jaw following accidental injury). Medicare Advantage plans have the flexibility to offer coverage of routine preventive and restorative dental services. Medicare dental coverage varies by type of Medicare Advantage plan selected by beneficiaries.[d]
Department of Veterans Affairs (VA)	VA coverage of dental services requires enrollment, and exact coverage of dental services varies by an individual veteran's status—for example, whether the veteran has a service-connected disability. In some instances, VA may provide comprehensive dental care, while in other cases covered dental services may be limited. For example, some veterans with service-connected disabilities are eligible for any necessary dental care. Other veterans are only eligible for dental care if their dental problems may complicate existing medical conditions.
Department of Defense TRICARE	TRICARE—the Department of Defense's regionally structured health care system—offers dental benefits as a separate program that for many beneficiaries requires separate enrollment. The TRICARE Dental Program and TRICARE Retiree Dental Program are voluntary and require enrollment. The TRICARE Active Duty Dental Program supplements services provided at military dental treatment facilities for active duty service members. Benefits vary by program and eligibility—for example, families may have to purchase a supplemental dental policy outside of their medical coverage to obtain dental coverage.

Source: GAO summary of agency information.

[a]Medicaid, a joint federal and state program that provides health care coverage for certain low-income individuals and families, provided health coverage for an estimated 70 million enrollees in fiscal year

2011. States operate their Medicaid programs within broad federal requirements and may contract with managed care organizations to provide Medicaid medical and dental benefits.

[b]States can administer their CHIP programs as (1) an expansion of their Medicaid program, (2) a stand-alone program, or (3) a combination of Medicaid expansion and stand-alone.

[c]Pub. L. No. 111-3, § 501, 123 Stat. 8, 84.

[d]Medicare Part A covers hospital and other inpatient stays. Medicare Part B is optional insurance and covers hospital outpatient, physician, and other services. Medicare beneficiaries have the option of obtaining coverage for Medicare Part A and B services from private health plans that participate in the Medicare Advantage program—also known as Medicare Part C. In 2010, about 25 percent of Medicare beneficiaries were enrolled in Medicare Advantage plans. Medicare Advantage is a private plan alternative to traditional Medicare fee-for-service and may provide benefits, such as dental coverage, not included in traditional Medicare fee-for-service.

Dental Care Provided by Health Centers

HHS's HRSA reported that in 2011, over 4 million patients used dental services at federally funded health centers.[16] Under the Health Center Program, health centers—which must be located in federally designated medically underserved areas or serve a federally designated medically underserved population—are required to provide pediatric dental screenings and preventive dental services, as well as emergency medical referrals, which may also result in the provision of dental services. Health centers may provide required services, including required dental services, directly or via formal contract or referral agreements. However, health centers are not required to provide a full range of dental services.

A health center must establish a fee schedule for its services that is consistent with locally prevailing rates and reflects the health center's reasonable costs of providing services. A health center must also establish a sliding fee schedule for individuals who earn annual incomes equal to or less than 200 percent of the FPL.[17] HRSA reported that in 2011, over 92 percent of the more than 20 million patients served by health centers nationwide had income less than or equal to 200 percent of the FPL (and were eligible for a sliding scale fee based on income and family size).[18]

---

[16]42 U.S.C. § 254b. Health centers are funded in part through grants under the Health Center Program—administered by HRSA—and provide comprehensive primary care services for the medically underserved.

[17]The 2013 federal poverty guidelines state that a family of four at 200 percent of the poverty level has an income of $47,100 per year.

[18]According to HRSA officials, data specific to dental patients were not available.

Dental Care under the Patient Protection and Affordable Care Act

The Patient Protection and Affordable Care Act (PPACA) has designated pediatric dental care as an essential health benefit that new health plans must cover in the new health care exchanges and the small-group and individual markets. Exchanges may allow plans to offer stand-alone dental coverage providing, at a minimum, pediatric dental care. Adult dental coverage is not included as an essential health benefit. Plans that have grandfathered status under the law are not required to offer pediatric dental coverage.[19] PPACA has the potential to change the benefits and out-of-pocket payments associated with dental coverage; however, the extent of these changes is uncertain.

National Survey Data Show That Rates of Dental Coverage and Use of Dental Services Remained Generally Unchanged from 1996 to 2010

The rate of individuals with dental coverage remained largely unchanged from 1996 to 2010; around 62 to 63 percent of the population had private or Medicaid or CHIP dental coverage. In addition, from 1996 to 2010, the percentage of individuals who had a dental visit remained about the same, around 41 to 43 percent.

Coverage of Dental Services Remained Relatively Unchanged from 1996 to 2010

Our analysis of MEPS data showed that overall, the rate of dental coverage—the percentage of individuals reporting that they had dental coverage through private insurance or Medicaid or CHIP—remained relatively unchanged from 1996 to 2010.[20] Specifically, in 1996, 62 percent of individuals reported having dental coverage, and in 2010, 63 percent reported having dental coverage. For about 10 to 12 percent

---

[19]Private health care plans in existence as of March 23, 2010, are considered grandfathered plans that do not have to comply with certain PPACA coverage requirements. However, plans may lose their grandfathered status if they cut benefits or increase beneficiary cost sharing.

[20]For purposes of this report, we refer to children in Medicaid and CHIP as children in Medicaid, because the MEPS data do not distinguish between children in Medicaid and CHIP.

of the population, including many individuals covered by Medicare and other federal health programs, dental coverage status is unknown.[21]

While the overall percentage of individuals with dental coverage generally stayed the same between 1996 and 2010, the percentages with private dental and without insurance coverage decreased and the percentage with Medicaid dental coverage increased. Specifically, the percentage of individuals with private coverage was 53 percent in 1996 and 50 percent in 2010 (see fig. 1). The percentage of individuals with dental coverage under Medicaid increased steadily in each of the years we examined, from 9 percent in 1996 to 13 percent in 2010. The percentage of individuals reporting that they did not have dental coverage decreased from 28 percent in 1996 to 25 percent in 2010, leaving at least one in four individuals with no dental coverage—approximately 76 million people—in 2010. For 10 to 12 percent of individuals in each year we examined, it is unknown whether they had dental coverage. These individuals reported having some type of health coverage, such as Medicare coverage, but the MEPS survey structure did not allow us to determine whether that health coverage included dental coverage.

---

[21]Most of these individuals reported having Medicare coverage. Traditional Medicare offers very limited dental benefits. Medicare Advantage plans may include dental coverage. In 2010, about 25 percent of Medicare beneficiaries were in a Medicare Advantage plan, but not all plans offer dental coverage or offer dental coverage as an optional benefit. Consequently, this conservative approach may result in overstating the "unknown" category and understating the "none" category.

Figure 1: Dental Coverage Status, 1996, 2004, and 2010

1996

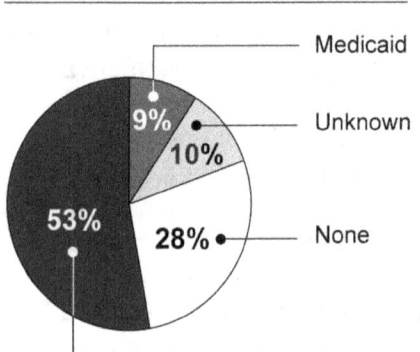

2004   2010

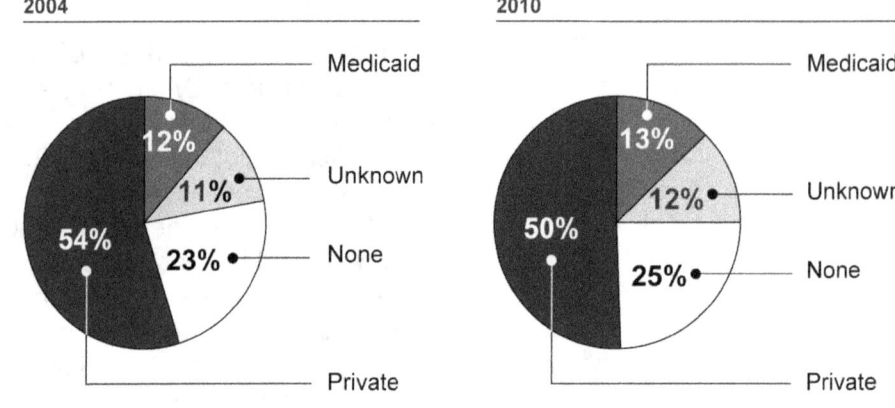

Source: GAO analysis of HHS data.

Notes: Data are from the Medical Expenditure Panel Survey (MEPS). This figure includes only the noninstitutionalized population. For 2004 and 2010, Medicaid includes children enrolled in the State Children's Health Insurance Program.

Individuals in the unknown category indicated that they had other types of public coverage, including state or federal programs such as Medicare or veteran's benefits. These programs might not have included dental coverage, or might have provided limited dental coverage to certain individuals. For these programs, the MEPS survey methodology did not allow us to identify which beneficiaries actually had dental coverage. Beneficiaries in these programs with a dental claim paid by private insurance during the period were counted as having private coverage. For example, Medicare Advantage enrollees who had a claim paid by private insurance were counted in the private insurance category. Medicare beneficiaries who did not have a claim paid by private insurance were included in the unknown category because they might have had dental coverage, such as under a Medicare Advantage plan, but did not use their coverage during the survey period.

Rates of private dental coverage among individuals in the high-income category (over 400 percent of FPL) were higher than any other income category in 1996, 2004 and 2010 (see fig. 2). Individuals in the poor-, low-, and middle-income groups saw a decline in the rates of private coverage over the same period.[22]

---

[22]For this analysis, poor individuals are individuals in families with income at or below 100 percent of the FPL. The low-income group is individuals in families with income at or below 200 percent of the FPL but above 100 percent of the FPL. Individuals in the middle-income group are those in families with income at or below 400 percent of the FPL, but above 200 percent of the FPL.

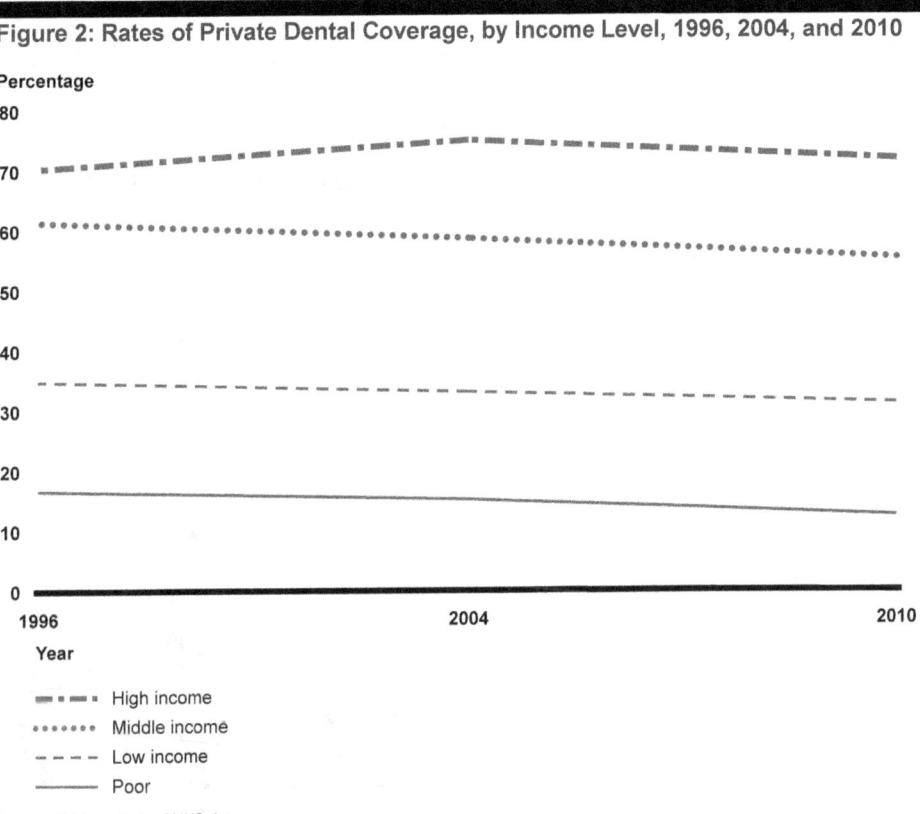

Figure 2: Rates of Private Dental Coverage, by Income Level, 1996, 2004, and 2010

Source: GAO analysis of HHS data.

Notes: Data are from the Medical Expenditure Panel Survey (MEPS). This figure includes only the noninstitutionalized population. Income is expressed in terms of poverty status. For this analysis, poor refers to individuals in families with income at or below 100 percent of the federal poverty level (FPL). The low-income group is individuals in families with income at or below 200 percent of the FPL but above 100 percent of the FPL. The middle-income group is individuals in families with income at or below 400 percent of the FPL but above 200 percent of the FPL. The high-income group is individuals in families with income greater than 400 percent of the FPL.

The percentage of individuals with Medicaid dental coverage increased from 9 percent in 1996 to 13 percent in 2010. This trend was largely driven by an increase in children covered by Medicaid, which requires pediatric dental coverage. The overall percentage of children (ages 0-20 years) reported to have dental coverage—through private coverage or Medicaid—increased from 72 percent (59 million) in 1996 to 81 percent (71 million) in 2010, and fewer children were uninsured, because more children were covered by Medicaid in 2010 than in prior years. The percentage of children with dental coverage through Medicaid increased from 18 percent (15 million) in 1996 to 33 percent (29 million) in 2010 (see fig. 3). This was the largest increase in coverage for any age group in Medicaid. The percentage of children with private dental

GAO-13-754 Dental Services Coverage and Payments

coverage decreased from 54 percent (44 million) in 1996 to 48 percent (42 million) in 2010. In addition, rates of children without dental coverage declined from 27 percent (22 million) to 17 percent (15 million) over the same period.

Figure 3: Dental Coverage Rates for Children, Ages 0-20 Years, 1996, 2004, and 2010

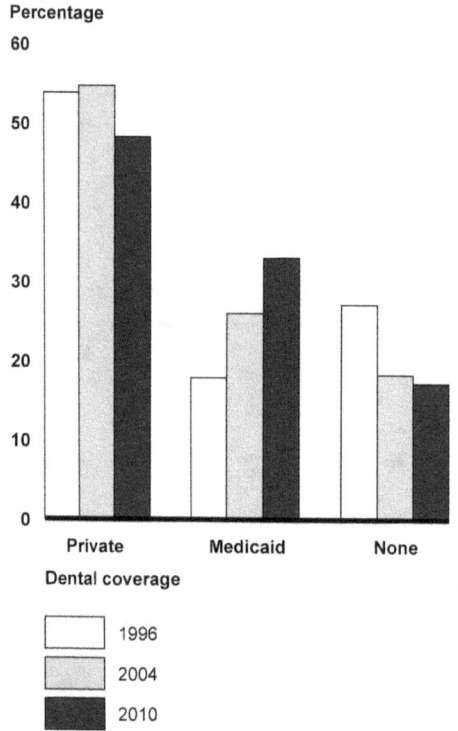

Source: GAO analysis of HHS data.

Notes: Data are from the Medical Expenditure Panel Survey (MEPS). This figure includes only the noninstitutionalized population. The unknown category for this age group is not reported in this figure because of small sample sizes (fewer than 2 percent of children ages 0-20 years were reported as having unknown dental coverage). For 2004 and 2010, Medicaid includes children enrolled in the State Children's Health Insurance Program.

Use of Dental Services Remained Relatively Unchanged from 1996 to 2010

The percentage of individuals who used dental services—those who reported having at least one dental visit during the year—remained relatively unchanged at around 40 percent from 1996 to 2010. Specifically, about 43 percent of individuals in 1996 and 41 percent in 2010 had a dental visit. Table 3 shows our analysis of MEPS data on the use of dental services.

Table 3: Percentage of Individuals with a Dental Visit, 1996, 2004, and 2010

	1996	2004	2010
Dental visit	42.9	43.6	41.3
No dental visit	57.1	56.4	58.7
Total	**100.0**	**100.0**	**100.0**

Source: GAO analysis of HHS data.

Notes: Data are from the Medical Expenditure Panel Survey (MEPS). This table includes only the noninstitutionalized population.

Trends in dental visits by individuals with private dental coverage largely explained why the percentage of individuals with a dental visit remained relatively unchanged from 1996 to 2010. Specifically, over this period the percentage of individuals with private dental coverage who had a dental visit remained the same, at around 56 percent (see table 4), and individuals with private coverage made up a large majority—around 80 to 85 percent—of the population with dental coverage during that time period. The number of individuals without dental coverage who had a dental visit declined—from 26 percent, or 19 million individuals, in 1996 to 18 percent, or 14 million individuals, in 2010.

Table 4: Percentage of Individuals with a Dental Visit, by Coverage Status, 1996, 2004, and 2010

	1996	2004	2010
Private	56.4	57.3	56.9
Medicaid	27.7	31.6	33.6
Unknown[a]	33.5	34.8	31.8
None	25.8	21.7	18.0

Source: GAO analysis of HHS data.

Notes: Data are from the Medical Expenditure Panel Survey (MEPS). This table includes only the noninstitutionalized population with a dental visit. For 2004 and 2010, Medicaid includes children enrolled in the State Children's Health Insurance Program.

[a]Individuals in the unknown category indicated that they had other types of public medical coverage, including state or federal programs such as Medicare or veteran's benefits. These programs might not have included dental coverage, or might have provided limited dental coverage to certain individuals. For these programs, the MEPS survey methodology did not allow us to identify which beneficiaries actually had dental coverage. Beneficiaries in these programs with a dental claim paid by insurance during the period were counted as having private coverage. For example, Medicare Advantage enrollees who had a claim paid by private insurance were counted in the private insurance category. Medicare beneficiaries who did not have a claim paid by insurance were included in the unknown category because they might have had dental coverage such as under a Medicare Advantage plan, but did not use their coverage during the survey period.

GAO-13-754 Dental Services Coverage and Payments

The percentage of individuals with Medicaid who had a dental visit increased from 1996 to 2010. This increase reflects an increase in the number of children with Medicaid coverage who had a dental visit, although these children still had dental visits at lower rates than privately insured children (58 percent). The percentage of children with Medicaid dental coverage with a dental visit increased from 28 percent, or 4 million children, in 1996 to 37 percent, or 11 million children, in 2010. (See fig. 4.)

Figure 4: Percentage of Children, Ages 0-20 Years, with Private and Medicaid Dental Coverage with a Dental Visit, 1996, 2004, and 2010

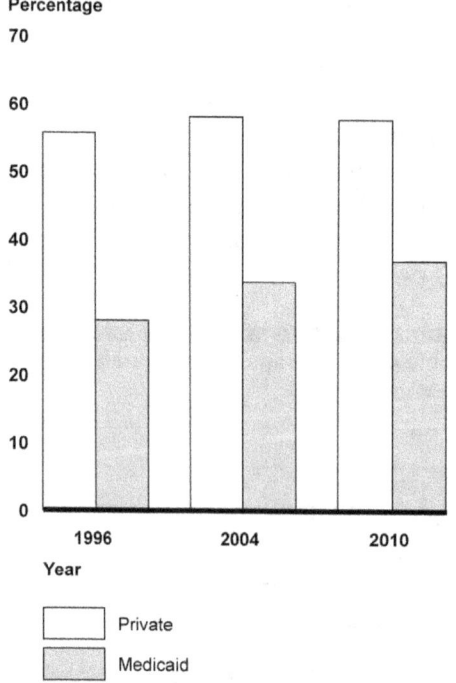

Source: GAO analysis of HHS data.

Notes: Data are from the Medical Expenditure Panel Survey (MEPS). This figure includes the noninstitutionalized population with a dental visit. From 1996 to 2010, 72 percent to 81 percent of children ages 0-20 years had private or Medicaid dental coverage. For 2004 and 2010, Medicaid includes children enrolled in the State Children's Health Insurance Program.

Among individuals who reported having a dental visit, there was an increase in the percentage reporting that they received diagnostic and preventive services (for example, exams and cleanings) and a decrease in those reporting that they received other services, such as restorative services (for example, fillings), from 1996 to 2010. Specifically, the percentage of visits for diagnostic and preventive services as a proportion

GAO-13-754 Dental Services Coverage and Payments

of total dental services increased (see fig. 5). Seventy-six percent of dental visits in 2010 consisted of diagnostic or preventive services (43 and 33 percent, respectively). This is an increase from 69 percent in 1996, when diagnostic and preventive services made up 40 and 29 percent of services received, respectively. The percentage of visits for other types of services decreased from 1996 to 2010. Specifically, restorative services—such as fillings—decreased slightly from 8 percent to 6 percent as a proportion of total dental services received in those years. Other services that decreased included prosthetic and orthodontic services.

Figure 5: Types of Dental Services as a Proportion of Total Services, 1996, 2004, and 2010

1996

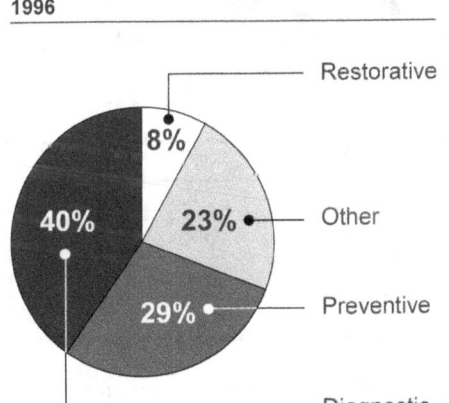

2004

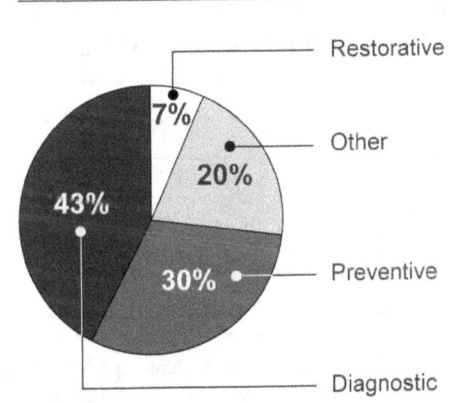

2010

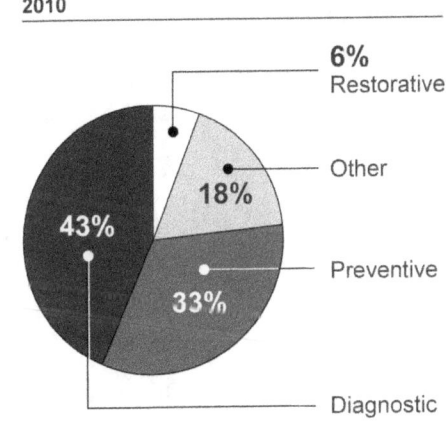

Source: GAO analysis of HHS data.

Notes: Data are from the Medical Expenditure Panel Survey (MEPS). This figure includes only the noninstitutionalized population and presents the percentage of visits that were for each category of dental procedure.

The "other" category includes treatment for temporomandibular joint and muscle disorders (jaw pain), bonding, whitening or bleaching, as well as periodontic, prosthetic, orthodontic, oral surgery, and endodontic services.

GAO-13-754 Dental Services Coverage and Payments

Average Payments for Dental Services Increased from 1996 to 2010

Average annual payments made on behalf of or by individuals for dental services—including payments from other payers such as insurers and out-of-pocket payments—increased from 1996 to 2010.[23] Average annual inflation-adjusted dental payments increased 26 percent from $520 per year in 1996 to $653 per year in 2010 (see table 5). The average annual payments made—including out-of-pocket payments and payments by other payers—increased 24 percent for the privately insured, 39 percent for individuals with Medicaid, and 38 percent for those without dental coverage. In addition, in 2010, average annual dental payments (out of pocket and payments made by other payers) for those with private coverage were nearly twice as much as the payments made by and on behalf of individuals with Medicaid coverage.

Table 5: Average Annual Dental Payments for Individuals with a Dental Visit, Adjusted for Inflation, by Coverage Status, 1996, 2004, and 2010

	1996	2004	2010
Average payment	$520	$647	$653
Private	580	713	719
Medicaid	269	356	373
Unknown[a]	—	623	630
None	406	528	561

Source: GAO analysis of HHS data.

Notes: Data are from the Medical Expenditure Panel Survey (MEPS). This table includes only the noninstitutionalized population with a dental visit. In MEPS, payments are defined as the sum of payments for care received, including out-of-pocket payments and payments made by private insurance, Medicaid, Medicare, and other payers. Payments were adjusted for inflation using the Consumer Price Index for All Urban Consumers (CPI-U), 2010 dollars. Dashes indicate the sample size was too small for a reliable estimate. For 2004 and 2010, Medicaid includes children enrolled in the State Children's Health Insurance Program.

[a]Individuals in the unknown category indicated that they had other types of public medical coverage, including state or federal programs such as Medicare or veteran's benefits. These programs might not have included dental coverage, or might have provided limited dental coverage to certain individuals. For these programs, the MEPS survey methodology did not allow us to identify which beneficiaries actually had dental coverage. Beneficiaries in these programs with a dental claim paid by insurance during the period were counted as having private coverage. For example, Medicare Advantage enrollees who had a claim paid by private insurance were counted in the private insurance category. Medicare beneficiaries who did not have a claim paid by insurance were included in the unknown category because they might have had dental coverage such as under a Medicare Advantage plan, but did not use their coverage during the survey period.

---

[23]In MEPS, payments are defined as the sum of payments for care received, including out-of-pocket payments and payments made by private insurance, Medicaid, and other payers. They do not include premium costs. Payments were adjusted for inflation using the Consumer Price Index for All Urban Consumers (CPI-U), 2010 dollars.

Average annual payments for dental services varied across income levels. Payments made by and on behalf of individuals in the low-, and middle-income groups increased steadily from 1996 to 2010. However, average annual payments made by and on behalf of individuals who were poor increased from $373 in 1996 to $493 in 2004, and then decreased to $437 in 2010.[24] For low-income individuals, that is, individuals with incomes at or below 200 percent but above 100 percent of the FPL, dental payments had the largest increase. Specifically, average annual dental payments for the low-income group increased from $393 in 1996 to $558 in 2010 (see fig. 6), about 42 percent. Average annual dental payments also increased for middle- and high-income individuals—23 and 25 percent, respectively.

[24]Poor includes individuals in families with income at or below 100 percent of the FPL.

Figure 6: Average Annual Payments for Dental Services for Individuals with a Dental Visit, Adjusted for Inflation, by Income Level, 1996, 2004, and 2010

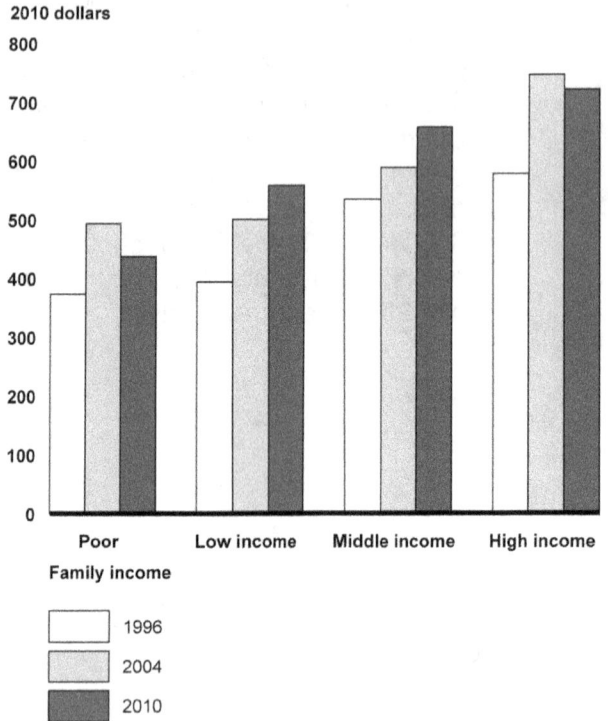

Source: GAO analysis of HHS data.

Notes: Data are from the Medical Expenditure Panel Survey (MEPS). This figure includes only the noninstitutionalized population with a dental visit. In MEPS, payments are defined as the sum of payments for care received, including out-of-pocket payments and payments made by private insurance, Medicaid, Medicare, and other sources. Payments were adjusted for inflation using the Consumer Price Index for All Urban Consumers (CPI-U), 2010 dollars.

For this analysis, poor are individuals in families with income at or below 100 percent of the federal poverty level (FPL). The low income group is individuals in families with incomes at or below 200 percent of the FPL but above 100 percent of the FPL. The middle-income group is individuals in families with income at or below 400 percent of the FPL but above 200 percent of the FPL. The high-income group is individuals in families with income greater than 400 percent of the FPL.

Individuals' out-of-pocket payments for dental services, separate from payments by other payers, when adjusted for inflation, generally increased from 1996 to 2010 (see fig. 7). Specifically, average annual out-of-pocket payments made by individuals with private coverage increased 21 percent from 1996 to 2010—from $242 to $294. Individuals with no dental coverage experienced the greatest increase in average annual out-of-pocket payments, from $392 to $518, a 32 percent increase. For individuals with Medicaid coverage, their average annual out-of-pocket payments remained relatively unchanged, $64 in 1996 and $59 in 2010.[25]

Figure 7: Average Annual Out-of-Pocket Payments for Individuals with a Dental Visit, 1996, 2004, and 2010

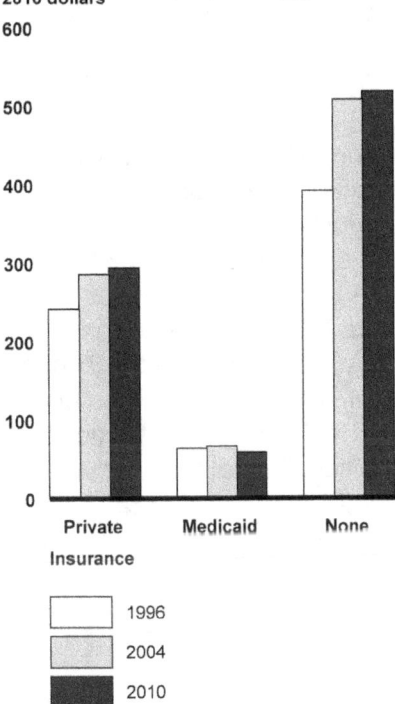

Source: GAO analysis of HHS data.

Notes: Data are from Medical Expenditure Panel Survey (MEPS). This table includes only the noninstitutionalized population with a dental visit. Payments were adjusted for inflation using the Consumer Price Index for All Urban Consumers (CPI-U), 2010 dollars. For 2004 and 2010, Medicaid includes children enrolled in the State Children's Health Insurance Program.

The out-of-pocket payments for individuals in the unknown group are not reported in the figure because of sample size concerns and high relative standard errors in the estimate. Relative standard error is the proportion of the standard error divided by the estimate itself.

[25]Cost sharing in Medicaid for most services is limited to nominal amounts. See http://www.medicaid.gov/Medicaid-CHIP-Program-Information/By-Topics/Cost-Sharing/Cost-Sharing.html (accessed May 24, 2013).

Fees Charged for Dental Services Varied between and within Communities

Dental fees charged by dentists and health centers varied across geographic areas and within communities. For 24 common dental procedures, dental fees charged by local dentists varied significantly between the 18 communities we examined. In addition, dental fees varied widely within communities. Dental fees also varied between local dentists and health centers that serve residents of the same community, but all health centers are required to offer sliding fee schedules for low-income individuals.

Dental Fees Varied Widely between Communities

For 24 common dental procedures, midpoint dental fees—the amount where half of fees charged were higher and half were lower—varied widely between the 18 communities we examined.[26] For example, midpoint dental fees for an adult prophylaxis (commonly called teeth cleaning) in large communities ranged from $76 in Nashville, Tennessee, to $155 in New York, New York. In smaller communities, midpoint fees ranged from $59 in Jackson, Tennessee, to $88 in Fresno, California (see fig. 8). Similarly, midpoint fees charged for a child prophylaxis ranged from $55 to $105 in large communities and $48 to $71 in small communities. Dental fees, as with other health care costs, vary by location. (See tables 10 to 27 in app. IV for more information on the range of dental fees for other common dental procedures in selected communities.)

---

[26]We analyzed dental insurance claims data in nine states corresponding to the nine U.S. Census divisions. Using 2010 Census data, we selected two communities in each state, one large, based on their population and volume of dental claims and one small based on population. Our nine selected community pairs, large and small (with selected geozip), were Phoenix (850) and Flagstaff (860), Arizona; Los Angeles (900) and Fresno (936), California; Miami (331) and Palm Coast (321), Florida; Chicago (606) and Champaign (618), Illinois; Boston (021) and Pittsfield (012), Massachusetts; Minneapolis (554) and Mankato (560), Minnesota; New York (100) and Elmira (148), New York; Nashville (372) and Jackson (382), Tennessee; and Dallas (752) and San Angelo (768), Texas. (See app. III for more information on our scope and methodology.)

Figure 8: Midpoint Dental Fees in 18 Communities for Teeth Cleaning (Adult and Child), 2012

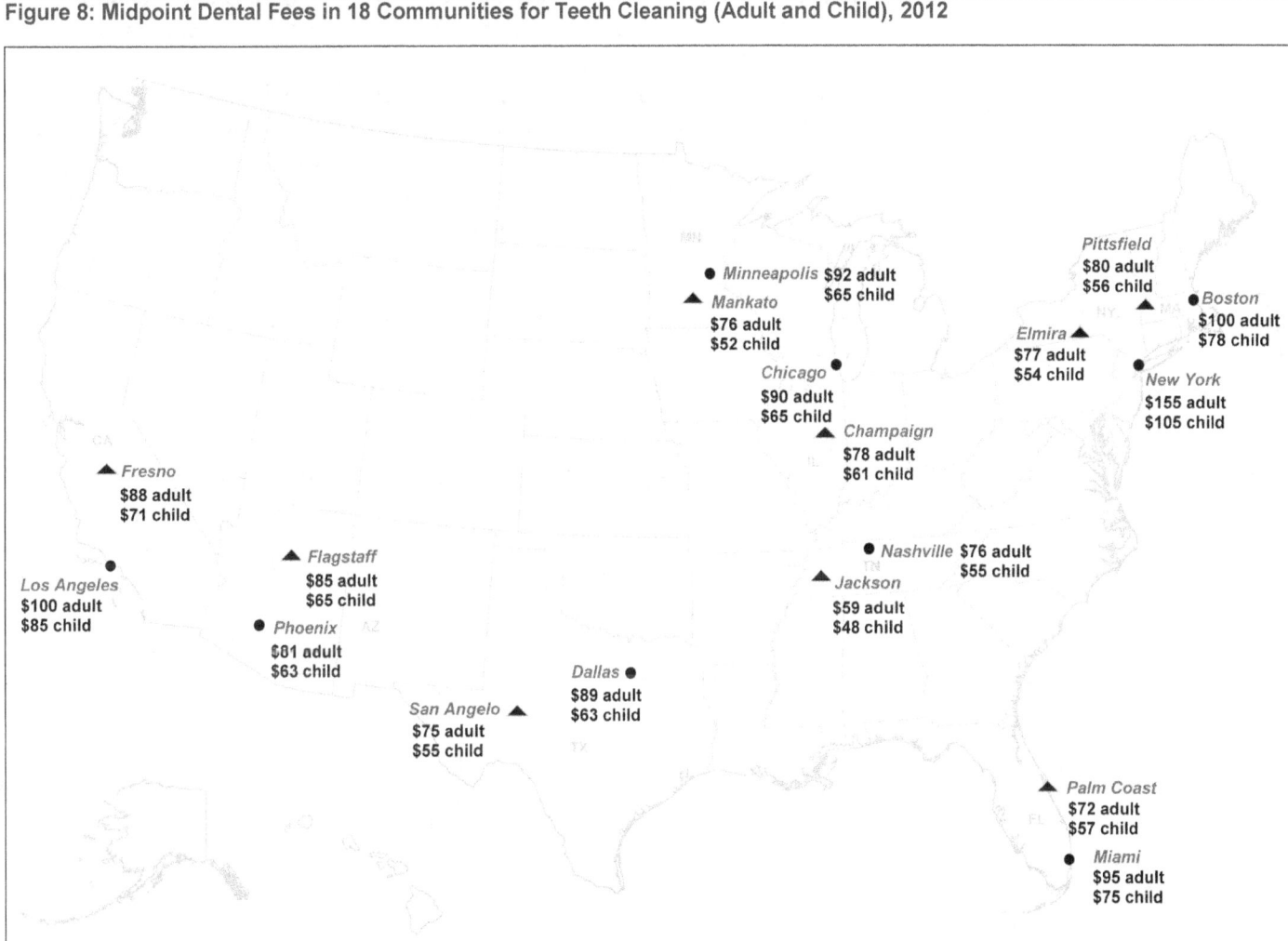

▲ Small communities

● Large communities

Source: GAO analysis of FAIR Health data; Map Resources (map).

Note: Fees are reported for Current Dental Terminology (CDT) codes D1110: Prophylaxis (Adult) and D1120: Prophylaxis (Child). The American Dental Association describes prophylaxis (commonly called teeth cleaning) as removal of plaque, calculus, and stains from the tooth structures in the permanent and transitional dentition.

Several factors can contribute to geographic variation in dental fees, including local wages and the cost of space and equipment needed to operate a practice. Although we identified no current peer-reviewed research that established a correlation between individual factors and the level of dental fees, geographic variation in spending for medical services

GAO-13-754 Dental Services Coverage and Payments

is well documented. For example, the Congressional Budget Office reported that a number of factors, including facilities, supplies, and wages, influence geographic variation in health care spending.[27] The Centers for Medicare & Medicaid Services (CMS), in setting Medicare payment rates for health care services, establishes a geographic practice cost index for each Medicare payment locality to account for variation in practice expenses. CMS reported that it did not have any comparable practice cost index for Medicaid dental fees.

Dental Fees Varied Widely within Communities

Dental claims data also showed significant differences within communities for all 24 common dental procedures we examined. Fees within the private practice dental setting are affected by local market conditions and decisions within the individually owned practices. FAIR Health dental claims data showed that within communities the difference between midpoint and upper-end fees was as high as 143 percent for localized delivery of antimicrobial agents. Upper-end fees were at least double the midpoint fees in at least one community for 8 of the 24 common procedures we examined (see table 6). (See app. IV for information on all 24 procedures in all 18 selected communities.)

---

[27]Congressional Budget Office, *Geographic Variation in Health Care Spending*, Pub. No. 2978 (Washington, D.C.: Feb. 2008).

GAO-13-754 Dental Services Coverage and Payments

Table 6: Procedures with the Largest Percentage Difference between Midpoint and Upper-End Fees, 2012

Current Dental Terminology (CDT) code	Description	Community (geozip)	Midpoint fee	Upper-end fee	Percentage difference
D4381	Localized Delivery of Antimicrobial Agents via a Controlled Release Vehicle Into Diseased Crevicular Tissue, per Tooth, by Report	Los Angeles, Calif. (900)	$80	$194	143%
D0120	Periodic Oral Evaluation – Established Patient	Miami, Fla. (331)	62	150	142
D0230	Radiographs/Diagnostic Imaging: Intraoral – Periapical Each Additional Film	New York, N.Y. (100)	21	50	138
D1203	Topical Application of Fluoride – Child	Los Angeles, Calif. (900)	40	90	125
D0274	Radiographs/Diagnostic Imaging: Bitewings – Four Films	Miami, Fla. (331)	66	140	112
D7140	Extraction, Erupted Tooth or Exposed Root (Elevation and/or Forceps Removal)	New York, N.Y. (100)	290	600	107
D0220	Radiographs/Diagnostic Imaging: Intraoral – Periapical First Film	Miami, Fla. (331)	25	50	100
D1204	Topical Application of Fluoride – Adult	Los Angeles, Calif. (900)	40	80	100

Source: GAO analysis of FAIR Health data (as of January 2013). American Dental Association (ADA) CDT definitions.

Note: Midpoint fees are the 50th percentile and upper-end fees are the 95th percentile (percentiles indicate the percentage of reported fees that are below the stated amount; for example, 95 percent of reported fees fall below the 95th percentile).

Dental fees within communities also varied widely for diagnostic procedures. For the most common diagnostic procedure, a periodic oral evaluation of an established patient, the percentage difference between reported midpoint and upper-end fees in large communities ranged from 20 percent to 142 percent (see table 7). For example, in Miami, Florida, half of the fees charged by dentists for a periodic oral examination of an established patient were $62 or less, but 5 percent of fees charged for that procedure were $150 or more, a 142 percent difference. In small communities, the percentage difference was less, ranging from 17 percent to 58 percent.

GAO-13-754 Dental Services Coverage and Payments

Table 7: Differences between Midpoint and Upper-End Dental Fees Charged for a Periodic Oral Evaluation of an Established Patient, by Local Dentists in 18 Communities in Nine States, 2012

Community (geozip)	Midpoint fee	Upper-end fee	Percentage difference
Large communities			
Miami, Fla. (331)	$62	$150	142%
New York, N.Y. (100)	80	152	90
Los Angeles, Calif. (900)	63	110	75
Chicago, Ill. (606)	49	72	47
Phoenix, Ariz. (850)	45	62	38
Nashville, Tenn. (372)	42	57	36
Boston, Mass. (021)	49	65	33
Dallas, Tex. (752)	47	61	30
Minneapolis, Minn. (554)	50	60	20
Small communities			
San Angelo, Tex. (768)	$38	$60	58
Fresno, Calif. (936)	45	66	47
Jackson, Tenn. (382)	33	45	36
Palm Coast, Fla. (321)	36	49	36
Pittsfield, Mass. (012)	36	47	31
Elmira, N.Y. (148)	40	52	30
Champaign, Ill. (618)	40	50	25
Mankato, Minn. (560)	41	48	17
Flagstaff, Ariz. (860)	47	55	17

Source: GAO analysis of FAIR Health data (as of January 2013). American Dental Association (ADA) Current Dental Terminology (CDT) definitions.

Notes: Fees are reported for CDT code D0120: Periodic Oral Evaluation (Established Patient). ADA describes this procedure as an evaluation performed on a patient of record to determine any changes in the patient's dental and medical health status since a previous comprehensive or periodic evaluation. This includes an oral cancer evaluation and periodontal screening where indicated, and may require interpretation of information acquired through additional diagnostic procedures.

Midpoint fees are the 50th percentile and upper-end fees are the 95th percentile (percentiles indicate the percentage of reported fees that are below the stated amount; for example, 95 percent of reported fees fall below the 95th percentile).

Dental fees within communities also varied widely for restorative procedures. For the most common restorative procedure, a filling, the percentage difference between reported midpoint and upper-end fees in large communities ranged from 19 percent to 67 percent (see table 8). For example, in Phoenix, Arizona, half of the fees charged by dentists for a filling were $195 or less, but 5 percent of fees charged for that procedure were $325 or more, a 67 percent difference. In small communities, the percentage difference was smaller, ranging from 13 percent to 38 percent.

Table 8: Differences between Midpoint and Upper-End Dental Fees Charged for a Filling by Local Dentists in 18 Communities in Nine States, 2012

Community (geozip)	Midpoint fee	Upper-end fee	Percentage difference
Large communities			
Phoenix, Ariz. (850)	$195	$325	67%
Miami, Fla. (331)	200	320	60
Dallas, Tex. (752)	189	294	56
Los Angeles, Calif. (900)	237	365	54
New York, N.Y. (100)	300	450	50
Nashville, Tenn. (372)	200	287	44
Chicago, Ill. (606)	205	290	41
Boston, Mass. (021)	225	301	34
Minneapolis, Minn. (554)	244	290	19
Small communities			
Fresno, Calif. (936)	$208	$288	38
Pittsfield, Mass. (012)	179	242	35
San Angelo, Tex. (768)	180	242	34
Palm Coast, Fla. (321)	175	231	32
Flagstaff, Ariz. (860)	206	266	29
Elmira, N.Y. (148)	179	230	28
Mankato, Minn. (560)	194	243	25
Jackson, Tenn. (382)	160	191	19
Champaign, Ill. (618)	208	235	13

Source: GAO analysis of FAIR Health data (as of January 2013). American Dental Association (ADA) Current Dental Terminology (CDT) definitions.

Notes: Fees are reported for CDT code D2392: Resin-Based Composite (Two Surfaces, Posterior). According to ADA, a resin-based composite refers to a broad category of materials including, but not limited to, composites. May include bonded composite, light-cured composite, etc. Tooth preparation, acid etching, adhesives (including resin-bonding agents), liners and bases and curing are included as part of the restoration.

Midpoint fees are the 50th percentile and upper-end fees are the 95th percentile (percentiles indicate the percentage of reported fees that are below the stated amount; for example, 95 percent of reported fees fall below the 95th percentile).

Dental fees also varied between midpoint fees of local dentists billing private insurers and the full fees of the federally funded health centers that serve residents of the same community.[28] In the 18 communities we examined, full dental fees for a tooth extraction (the most common oral surgery procedure) were typically lower at health centers. For patients with incomes at or below 100 percent of the FPL, 10 health centers offered a 100 percent fee discount and 8 health centers had fees ranging from $16 to $148 for extracting a tooth (see table 9). Health centers' full fees—which fewer than 8 percent of health center patients pay—were often, but not always, lower than the midpoint fees charged by local dentists. In some cases, midpoint fees charged by local dentists were higher than health center fees by a wide margin. For example, in Los Angeles, the midpoint fee charged by local dentists for a tooth extraction was nearly 3 times the full fee charged by a health center serving residents of the same community. In other cases, full fees were higher than those of local dentists. For example, in Fresno the health center's full fee was $177 for a tooth extraction compared to the midpoint fee charged by local dentists of $142. (See app. IV for additional information on local dentist fees and health center dental fees.)

[28]For families that cannot afford the prevailing cost of dental care, many obtain dental care from federally funded health centers. Dental services provided at health centers are available to all patients, regardless of their ability to pay, and in general, health centers must offer discounted fees for families with incomes at or below 200 percent of the FPL.

Table 9: Dental Fees Charged for a Tooth Extraction by Local Dentists and Health Centers in 18 Communities in Nine States, 2012

Community (geozip)	Local dentists' midpoint fee[a]	Health centers[b]	
		Full fee	100% of federal poverty level (FPL)
Large communities			
New York, N.Y. (100)	$290	$229	$36
Boston, Mass. (021)	175	157	0
Minneapolis, Minn. (554)	167	147	0
Miami, Fla. (331)	165	166	70
Los Angeles, Calif. (900)	157	54	0
Dallas, Tex. (752)	152	159	16
Chicago, Ill. (606)	150	105	0
Phoenix, Ariz. (850)	125	132	35
Nashville, Tenn. (372)	125	70	0
Small communities			
Champaign, Ill. (618)	$159	$106	[c]
Pittsfield, Mass. (012)	153	145	0
Flagstaff, Ariz. (860)	149	179	90
Elmira, N.Y. (148)	143	122	0
Fresno, Calif. (936)	142	177	0
San Angelo, Tex. (768)	137	148	148[d]
Palm Coast, Fla. (321)	135	134	0
Mankato, Minn. (560)	132	122	0
Jackson, Tenn. (382)	97	[e]	[f]

Source: GAO analysis of FAIR Health and health center data (as of January 2013). American Dental Association (ADA) Current Dental Terminology (CDT) definitions.

Note: Fees are reported for CDT code D7140: Extraction, Erupted Tooth or Exposed Root (Elevation and/or Forceps Removal). ADA describes this procedure as including routine removal of tooth structure, minor smoothing of socket bone, and closure, as necessary.

[a]Midpoint fees are the 50th percentile reported for the procedure in the geozip (percentiles indicate the percentage of reported fees that are below the stated amount; for example, 50 percent of reported fees fall below the 50th percentile).

[b]Generally, full fees are those charged by health centers for patients with incomes above 200 percent of the FPL or those with private coverage. Fees at 100 percent of the FPL are charged by health centers for patients with income at or less than 100 percent of the FPL.

[c]For patients at or below 100 percent of the FPL, the health center combines multiple services for a discounted fee. For example; patients would pay a $40 copayment for a restorative appointment (on one or more teeth) which could include a tooth extraction.

[d]Health center does not discount this procedure.

[e]Health center does not provide/subsidize dental care for patients with income at or above 200 percent of the FPL.

[Health center does not operate an in-house dental program, but contracts for dental care with a local dentist. Dental patients with income below 200 percent of the FPL are charged a $20 copayment, and can receive up to $150 worth of dental services per year.

To assist health centers in establishing sliding fee schedules for low-income patients, HRSA officials told us that, as of June 2013, they were in the process of preparing guidance on discounting fees for all services provided as part of a health center's scope of project, including dental services. In technical comments on a draft of this report, HHS noted that the draft guidance was in final clearance, indicating that it was uncertain whether the final policy would include guidance on establishing full-fee schedules. According to HHS, there is often a significant unmet need for dental care services among patients served by health centers and as a result, health centers and their community boards must make decisions about whether to provide additional dental services to meet this need and develop a fee schedule consistent with Health Center Program requirements. HHS commented that variation in fees and discounts reflect each health center's unique community characteristics as well as the board's decision on how best to balance their ability to provide these services against the unmet need in their community.

Agency Comments

HHS reviewed a draft of this report and provided technical comments, which we incorporated as appropriate.

As agreed with your office, unless you publicly announce the contents of this report earlier, we plan no further distribution until 30 days from the report date. At that time, we will send copies to the Secretary of Health and Human Services, interested congressional committees, and others. In addition, the report will be available at no charge on the GAO website at http://www.gao.gov.

If you or your staff have any questions about this report, please contact me at (202) 512-7114 or iritanik@gao.gov. Contact points for our Offices of Congressional Relations and Public Affairs may be found on the last page of this report. GAO staff who made major contributions to this report are listed in appendix V.

Sincerely yours,

Katherine Iritani
Director, Health Care

Appendix I: National Dental Expenditures

To determine national trends in U.S. dental expenditures, we obtained national expenditure data from HHS's Centers for Medicare & Medicaid Services' (CMS) Office of the Actuary. In 2011, national expenditures for dental services in the United States were about $108 billion, an inflation-adjusted increase from $64 billion in 1996 (see fig. 9). Inflation-adjusted expenditures in the United States for dental services rose an average of 3.6 percent per year between 1996 and 2011—ranging from a 0.8 percent decrease in 2009 to a 6.9 percent increase in 2002.

Figure 9: National Expenditures for Dental Services, Adjusted for Inflation, 1996-2011

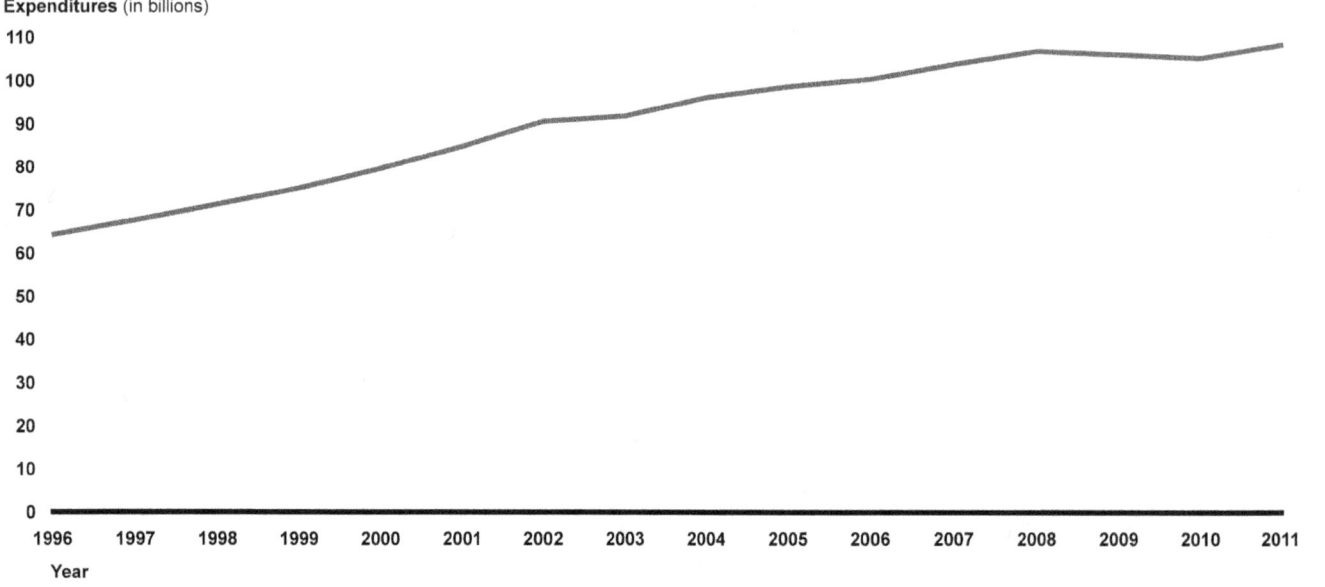

Source: GAO analysis of CMS Office of the Actuary data.

Notes: Data are from the National Health Expenditure Accounts. The expenditures in this figure have been adjusted to 2011 dollars using the 2011 Gross Domestic Product index and conversion factors.

Appendix II: Urban and Rural Dental Visit Rates

Individuals who lived in urban and rural areas reported dental visits at different rates, with individuals in urban areas reporting higher rates of dental visits. For example, in all age groups, fewer individuals in rural areas reported having a dental visit than individuals in urban areas (see fig. 10). Specifically, 34 percent of individuals ages 65 and older living in rural areas had dental visits in a year, compared with 45 percent of their counterparts in urban areas, for 2008 through 2010. The rates for children were similar: 35 percent of children 0 to 20 years old living in rural areas reported a dental visit in a year, compared with 45 percent of children in urban areas.

Figure 10: Percentage of Individuals with a Dental Visit, by Age and Location, 2008-2010

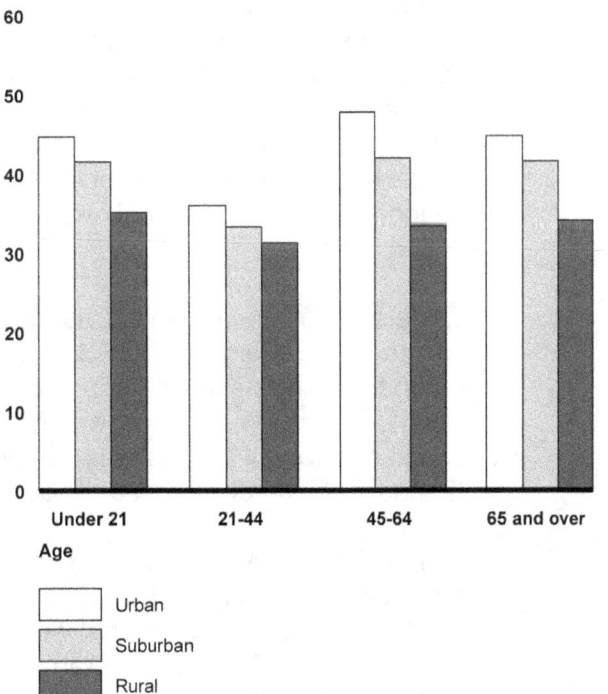

Source: GAO analysis of HHS data.

Notes: Data are from the Medical Expenditure Panel Survey (MEPS). This figure includes the noninstitutionalized population with a dental visit during the year and reflects 3 years of MEPS data to ensure adequate sample sizes for reporting. The categories are based on the size of the urbanized population in counties; the nonmetropolitan counties are separated into those that are adjacent to metropolitan areas (suburban) and those that are more remote (rural).

Appendix III: Scope and Methodology

To provide information on the trends in dental coverage rates, use of dental services, and payments by individuals and other payers for dental services, we analyzed nationwide data from the Medical Expenditure Panel Survey (MEPS). We examined and analyzed data from 3 years: 1996, 2004, and 2010. We selected these years for our analysis because 1996 was the first year MEPS was administered and 2010 was the most recent year for which data were available, we included 2004 to provide three points in time for our analysis. MEPS is administered by the Department of Health and Human Services' (HHS) Agency for Healthcare Research and Quality (AHRQ) and is a nationally representative survey of the noninstitutionalized population, including families, medical providers, and employers. MEPS collects self-reported information on individuals' demographics, health and insurance status, and use of medical services by setting and provider type, as well as expenses and payments related to those medical and dental visits, among other things. We analyzed responses to MEPS questions about types of dental insurance coverage, number of dental visits, types of dental procedures received, and payments made related to those visits. A dental visit refers to care by or visits to any type of dental care provider, including general dentists, dental hygienists, dental technicians, dental surgeons, orthodontists, endodontists, and periodontists. For this report, we referred to all visits as dental visits.

To determine whether an individual had private dental insurance coverage, we examined MEPS data and noted whether the individual reported having dental insurance or had private insurance pay on a dental claim during the year. Thus, we considered an individual to have private dental coverage if he or she (1) reported having dental insurance or (2) had that insurer pay on a dental claim.

To identify adult Medicaid coverage by state, we used a list of states provided by the Centers for Medicare & Medicaid Services (CMS) for 2004 and 2010. For states that were identified as having "limited" or "emergency only" dental coverage, we did not consider those benefits to be Medicaid dental coverage. Our analysis of adult Medicaid coverage based on the list from CMS resulted in only small differences from a similar analysis conducted by AHRQ for its Chartbook 17 publication that examines dental coverage and expenses.[1]

To categorize dental procedure codes, we consulted with AHRQ and used the same categories used by AHRQ for its Chartbook 17. For example, AHRQ placed various dental procedure codes related to preventive dental care—such as teeth cleaning and sealant application—in the preventive services category.

In MEPS, expenses are defined as the sum of payments for care received, including out-of-pocket payments and payments made by private insurance, Medicaid, Medicare, and other sources. For this report, we referred to MEPS expenses as payments—payments by insurers or other payers as well as out-of-pocket payments made by individuals. To present the dental payments in constant 2010 dollars, we used the Consumer Price Index for All Urban Consumers (CPI-U) as the price deflator for both the aggregate dental payments and the out-of-pocket payments.

To identify potential differences in dental service use and payments by demographic groups, we looked at responses by age group, income level, and urban or rural area. We examined income level in terms of the federal poverty level. To conduct the urban and rural analysis, we assigned individuals to one of three groups based on the county they lived in—each county was designated urban, suburban, or rural based on the Rural Urban Continuum Codes (RUCC).[2] We categorized those individuals as follows: those who lived in counties designated 1, 2, or 3 in the RUCC were urban; counties designated 4, 6, or 8, suburban; and in counties designated 5, 7, or 9, rural.

In conducting the urban and rural analysis, to ensure adequate sample sizes, we combined MEPS data for 2008, 2009, and 2010. This was the

---

[1]Chartbook 17 examined MEPS data related to dental coverage, use and payments in 1996 and 2004. To calculate Medicaid coverage for 1996, we used AHRQ's information used in the Chartbook. R.J. Manski and E. Brown, *Dental Use, Expenses, Private Dental Coverage, and Changes, 1996 and 2004*, MEPS Chartbook No.17 (Rockville, Md.: Agency for Healthcare Research and Quality, 2007). See http://www.meps.ahrq.gov/mepsweb/data_files/publications/cb17/cb17.pdf.

[2]For this analysis, we used the 2003 RUCCs. This was the most recent data available at the time of our study.

only analysis where a combination of years was necessary. Despite this effort, small sample sizes for some analyses limited the reliability of the results, and in those cases, we did not report those analyses.

To determine the reliability of the MEPS data, we reviewed related documentation, interviewed agency officials, and identified other studies that used MEPS to address similar research questions to compare the published data with our findings. We determined that the MEPS data were sufficiently reliable for the purposes of our report.

To determine the extent to which dental fees varied between and within selected communities, we analyzed dental insurance claims data and dental fees charged by selected health centers in nine states corresponding to the nine U.S. Census Bureau divisions. Using 2010 Census data, we selected two communities in each state, one large based on population and volume of dental claims and one small based on population. Our nine selected community pairs, large and small (with selected geozips), were Phoenix (850) and Flagstaff (860), Arizona; Los Angeles (900) and Fresno (936), California; Miami (331) and Palm Coast (321), Florida; Chicago (606) and Champaign (618), Illinois; Boston (021) and Pittsfield (012), Massachusetts; Minneapolis (554) and Mankato (560), Minnesota; New York (100) and Elmira (148), New York; Nashville (372) and Jackson (382), Tennessee; and Dallas (752) and San Angelo (768), Texas.

To identify representative dental fees in each community, we analyzed (1) 2012 dental insurance claims data compiled by FAIR Health, Inc., as of January 2013,[3] and (2) dental fee schedules from selected health centers serving these communities. Based on the FAIR Health claims data, we selected 24 of the most of commonly billed dental procedures in six categories of the American Dental Association's (ADA) Current Dental Terminology (CDT) codes: five diagnostic, five preventive, five restorative, three endodontic, three periodontic, and three oral surgery.[4] We consulted with academic dental experts and ADA officials to confirm that

---

[3]The FAIR Health data set contained information on 579 Current Dental Terminology (CDT) codes in 491 "geozips"—a geozip is an area that shares the first three digits of a postal zip code. See http://www.fairhealth.org/ for more information about FAIR Health and the dental claims data set.

[4]Codes on Dental Procedures and Nomenclature are the intellectual property of the ADA as copyright owner.

the CDT codes we selected were representative of common dental procedures. We also compared our list of common dental procedures to data from the ADA Survey of Dental Fees.[5] We also obtained health center dental fees for these 24 procedures in our 18 selected communities. Based on a list of health centers provided by HHS's Health Resources and Services Administration (HRSA), we selected one health center (the center that served the most dental patients) in each community. We obtained full-fee and sliding fee schedules from each health center, although some health centers did not provide or bill separately for all 24 procedures. The 18 health centers studied may not be representative of the more than 1,200 health centers supported by HRSA.

For each selected dental procedure, we extracted from the FAIR Health data set the midpoint dental fee (the 50th percentile) and the upper-end fee (the 95th percentile). A percentile indicates the percentage of reported fees that were below the stated amount; for example, 95 percent of reported fees fall below the 95th percentile. Within each community, we selected one geozip (an area that shares the first three digits of a postal zip code) with the most dental claims to represent the community. Because geozip boundaries do not align with metropolitan statistical area designations, we selected one geozip (the one with the most dental claims) to represent each large and each small metropolitan area. Large metropolitan areas can include multiple geozips. For example, the Los Angeles/Long Beach metropolitan area includes geozips 900 to 912 (excluding 909).

To determine the reliability of the FAIR Health and health center data, we reviewed related documentation, interviewed agency officials and academic experts, and conducted data testing for missing data. We determined that both the FAIR Health and health center data were sufficiently reliable for the purposes of our report.

---

[5]American Dental Association, *2011 Survey of Dental Fees* (Chicago, Ill.: December 2011).

Appendix IV: Dental Fees Charged for Common Dental Procedures in 18 Communities

This appendix presents information on local dentist fees and health center fees for 24 common dental procedures in the 18 communities (by specific geozips) we examined (see tables 10 to 27).

Table 10: Dental Fees Charged for Common Procedures in Phoenix, Arizona (850), 2012

CDT code	Description	Local dentist fee		Health center fee	
		Midpoint[a]	Upper-end[b]	100% FPL[c]	Full fee[d]
Diagnostic					
D0120	Periodic Oral Evaluation – Established Patient	$45	$62	$35	$42
D0150	Comprehensive Oral Evaluation – New or Established Patient	75	95	35	72
D0220	Radiographs/Diagnostic Imaging: Intraoral – Periapical First Film	25	35	24	24
D0230	Radiographs/Diagnostic Imaging: Intraoral – Periapical Each Additional Film	20	29	20	20
D0274	Radiographs/Diagnostic Imaging: Bitewings – Four Films	53	71	35	52
Preventive					
D1110	Prophylaxis – Adult	81	99	35	74
D1120	Prophylaxis – Child	63	77	35	56
D1203	Topical Application of Fluoride – Child	30	40	30	30
D1204	Topical Application of Fluoride – Adult	30	40	32	32
D1351	Sealant – per Tooth	46	56	35	46
Restorative					
D2330	Resin-Based Composite – One Surface, Anterior	141	190	35	128
D2391	Resin-Based Composite – One Surface, Posterior	155	219	35	144
D2392	Resin-Based Composite – Two Surfaces, Posterior	195	325	35	188
D2393	Resin-Based Composite – Three Surfaces, Posterior	237	363	35	234
D2950	Core Buildup, Including Any Pins	230	310	35	224
Endodontics					
D3310	Endodontic Therapy, Anterior Tooth (Excluding Final Restoration)	677	950	200	586
D3320	Endodontic Therapy, Bicuspid Tooth (Excluding Final Restoration)	789	1,000	300	686
D3330	Endodontic Therapy, Molar (Excluding Final Restoration)	1,045	1,250	400	840

CDT code	Description	Local dentist fee		Health center fee	
		Midpoint[a]	Upper-end[b]	100% FPL[c]	Full fee[d]
Periodontics					
D4341	Periodontal Scaling and Root Planing – Four or More Teeth per Quadrant	232	287	35	204
D4381	Localized Delivery of Antimicrobial Agents via a Controlled Release Vehicle Into Diseased Crevicular Tissue, per Tooth, by Report	45	104	[e]	[e]
D4910	Periodontal Maintenance	122	175	35	116
Oral surgery					
D7140	Extraction, Erupted Tooth or Exposed Root (Elevation and/or Forceps Removal)	125	195	35	132
D7210	Surgical Removal of Erupted Tooth Requiring Removal of Bone and/or Sectioning of Tooth, and Including Elevation of the Mucoperlosteal Flap if Indicated	240	300	35	224
D7240	Removal of Impacted Tooth – Completely Bony	400	490	[e]	[e]

Source: GAO analysis of FAIR Health and health center data (as of January 2013).

Note: Current Dental Terminology (CDT) Codes on Dental Procedures and Nomenclature are the intellectual property of the American Dental Association (ADA) as copyright owner.

[a]Midpoint fees are the 50th percentile (percentiles indicate the percentage of reported fees that are below the stated amount; for example, 50 percent of reported fees fall below the 50th percentile).

[b]Upper-end fees are the 95th percentile.

[c]100 percent federal poverty level (FPL) are fees charged by the health center for patients with income at or less than 100 percent of the FPL.

[d]Full fees are those charged by the health center for patients with income above 200 percent of FPL or for those with private coverage.

[e]Health center does not provide or bill separately for this procedure.

GAO-13-754 Dental Services Coverage and Payments

Table 11: Dental Fees Charged for Common Procedures in Flagstaff, Arizona (860), 2012

CDT code	Description	Local dentist fee		Health center fee	
		Midpoint[a]	Upper-end[b]	100 FPL[c]	Full fee[d]
Diagnostic					
D0120	Periodic Oral Evaluation – Established Patient	$47	$55	$26	$52
D0150	Comprehensive Oral Evaluation – New or Established Patient	78	99	44	88
D0220	Radiographs/Diagnostic Imaging: Intraoral – Periapical First Film	26	34	17	34
D0230	Radiographs/Diagnostic Imaging: Intraoral – Periapical Each Additional Film	22	27	12	24
D0274	Radiographs/Diagnostic Imaging: Bitewings – Four Films	59	70	45	90
Preventive					
D1110	Prophylaxis – Adult	85	99	47	94
D1120	Prophylaxis – Child	65	68	34	68
D1203	Topical Application of Fluoride – Child	34	38	20	40
D1204	Topical Application of Fluoride – Adult	28	40	24	48
D1351	Sealant – per Tooth	50	55	28.5	57
Restorative					
D2330	Resin-Based Composite – One Surface, Anterior	149	168	84.5	169
D2391	Resin-Based Composite – One Surface, Posterior	160	195	93.5	187
D2392	Resin-Based Composite – Two Surfaces, Posterior	206	266	131.5	263
D2393	Resin-Based Composite – Three Surfaces, Posterior	255	328	163.5	327
D2950	Core Buildup, Including Any Pins	250	309	138.5	277
Endodontics					
D3310	Endodontic Therapy, Anterior Tooth (Excluding Final Restoration)	700	825	400	800
D3320	Endodontic Therapy, Bicuspid Tooth (Excluding Final Restoration)	750	955	437.5	875
D3330	Endodontic Therapy, Molar (Excluding Final Restoration)	1,100	1,169	578.5	1,157
Periodontics					
D4341	Periodontal Scaling and Root Planing – Four or More Teeth per Quadrant	236	305	172.5	345
D4381	Localized Delivery of Antimicrobial Agents via a Controlled Release Vehicle Into Diseased Crevicular Tissue, per Tooth, by Report	49	60	[e]	[e]
D4910	Periodontal Maintenance	130	159	69	138

CDT code	Description	Local dentist fee		Health center fee	
		Midpoint[a]	Upper-end[b]	100 FPL[c]	Full fee[d]
Oral surgery					
D7140	Extraction, Erupted Tooth or Exposed Root (Elevation and/or Forceps Removal)	149	185	89.5	179
D7210	Surgical Removal of Erupted Tooth Requiring Removal of Bone and/or Sectioning of Tooth, and Including Elevation of the Mucoperlosteal Flap if Indicated	250	319	142.5	285
D7240	Removal of Impacted Tooth – Completely Bony	350	395	[e]	[e]

Source: GAO analysis of FAIR Health and health center data (as of January 2013).

Note: Current Dental Terminology (CDT) Codes on Dental Procedures and Nomenclature are the intellectual property of the American Dental Association (ADA) as copyright owner.

[a]Midpoint fees are the 50th percentile (percentiles indicate the percentage of reported fees that are below the stated amount; for example, 50 percent of reported fees fall below the 50th percentile).

[b]Upper-end fees are the 95th percentile.

[c]100 percent federal poverty level (FPL) are fees charged by the health center for patients with income at or less than 100 percent of the FPL.

[d]Full fees are those charged by the health center for patients with income above 200 percent of the FPL or for those with private coverage.

[e]Health center does not provide or bill separately for this procedure.

Table 12: Dental Fees Charged for Common Procedures in Los Angeles, California (900), 2012

CDT code	Description	Local dentist fee		Health center fee	
		Midpoint[a]	Upper-end[b]	100% FPL[c]	Full fee[d]
Diagnostic					
D0120	Periodic Oral Evaluation – Established Patient	$63	$110	$0	$150
D0150	Comprehensive Oral Evaluation – New or Established Patient	89	150	0	200
D0220	Radiographs/Diagnostic Imaging: Intraoral – Periapical First Film	30	50	e	e
D0230	Radiographs/Diagnostic Imaging: Intraoral – Periapical Each Additional Film	20	40	e	e
D0274	Radiographs/Diagnostic Imaging: Bitewings – Four Films	70	100	e	e
Preventive					
D1110	Prophylaxis – Adult	100	150	0	120
D1120	Prophylaxis – Child	85	120	0	90
D1203	Topical Application of Fluoride – Child	40	90	0	54
D1204	Topical Application of Fluoride – Adult	40	80	0	18
D1351	Sealant – per Tooth	66	102	0	66
Restorative					
D2330	Resin-Based Composite – One Surface, Anterior	163	290	0	165
D2391	Resin-Based Composite – One Surface, Posterior	185	300	0	117
D2392	Resin-Based Composite – Two Surfaces, Posterior	237	365	0	144
D2393	Resin-Based Composite – Three Surfaces, Posterior	280	414	0	171
D2950	Core Buildup, Including Any Pins	250	390	e	e
Endodontics					
D3310	Endodontic Therapy, Anterior Tooth (Excluding Final Restoration)	690	1,200	e	e
D3320	Endodontic Therapy, Bicuspid Tooth (Excluding Final Restoration)	800	1,400	e	e
D3330	Endodontic Therapy, Molar (Excluding Final Restoration)	1,000	1,700	0	500
Periodontics					
D4341	Periodontal Scaling and Root Planing – Four or More Teeth per Quadrant	240	350	0	84
D4381	Localized Delivery of Antimicrobial Agents via a Controlled Release Vehicle Into Diseased Crevicular Tissue, per Tooth, by Report	80	194	e	e
D4910	Periodontal Maintenance	145	195	0	72

CDT code	Description	Local dentist fee		Health center fee	
		Midpoint[a]	Upper-end[b]	100% FPL[c]	Full fee[d]
Oral surgery					
D7140	Extraction, Erupted Tooth or Exposed Root (Elevation and/or Forceps Removal)	157	300	0	54
D7210	Surgical Removal of Erupted Tooth Requiring Removal of Bone and/or Sectioning of Tooth, and Including Elevation of the Mucoperlosteal Flap if Indicated	275	495	0	96
D7240	Removal of Impacted Tooth – Completely Bony	450	754	[e]	[e]

Source: GAO analysis of FAIR Health and health center data (as of January 2013).

Note: Current Dental Terminology (CDT) Codes on Dental Procedures and Nomenclature are the intellectual property of the American Dental Association (ADA) as copyright owner.

[a]Midpoint fees are the 50th percentile (percentiles indicate the percentage of reported fees that are below the stated amount; for example, 50 percent of reported fees fall below the 50th percentile).

[b]Upper-end fees are the 95th percentile.

[c]For patients with income at or below 100 percent of the federal poverty level (FPL), fees are discounted 100 percent.

[d]Full fees are those charged by the health center for patients with income above 200 percent of the FPL or for those with private coverage.

[e]Health center does not provide or bill separately for this procedure.

Table 13: Dental Fees Charged for Common Procedures in Fresno, California (936), 2012

CDT code	Description	Local dentist fee		Health center fee	
		Midpoint[a]	Upper-end[b]	100% FPL[c]	Full fee[d]
Diagnostic					
D0120	Periodic Oral Evaluation – Established Patient	$45	$66	$0	$53
D0150	Comprehensive Oral Evaluation – New or Established Patient	72	107	0	93
D0220	Radiographs/Diagnostic Imaging: Intraoral – Periapical First Film	27	40	0	30
D0230	Radiographs/Diagnostic Imaging: Intraoral – Periapical Each Additional Film	17	30	0	26
D0274	Radiographs/Diagnostic Imaging: Bitewings – Four Films	60	83	0	68
Preventive					
D1110	Prophylaxis – Adult	88	108	0	95
D1120	Prophylaxis – Child	71	91	0	71
D1203	Topical Application of Fluoride – Child	30	50	0	39
D1204	Topical Application of Fluoride – Adult	31	50	0	39
D1351	Sealant – per Tooth	50	75	0	57
Restorative					
D2330	Resin-Based Composite – One Surface, Anterior	148	194	0	171
D2391	Resin-Based Composite – One Surface, Posterior	160	225	0	189
D2392	Resin-Based Composite – Two Surfaces, Posterior	208	288	0	246
D2393	Resin-Based Composite – Three Surfaces, Posterior	248	364	0	303
D2950	Core Buildup, Including Any Pins	225	325	0	289
Endodontics					
D3310	Endodontic Therapy, Anterior Tooth (Excluding Final Restoration)	650	895	0	785
D3320	Endodontic Therapy, Bicuspid Tooth (Excluding Final Restoration)	775	979	0	905
D3330	Endodontic Therapy, Molar (Excluding Final Restoration)	1,013	1,218	0	1,095
Periodontics					
D4341	Periodontal Scaling and Root Planing – Four or More Teeth per Quadrant	225	311	0	269
D4381	Localized Delivery of Antimicrobial Agents via a Controlled Release Vehicle Into Diseased Crevicular Tissue, per Tooth, by Report	91	150	[e]	[e]
D4910	Periodontal Maintenance	138	173	0	147

GAO-13-754 Dental Services Coverage and Payments

CDT code	Description	Local dentist fee		Health center fee	
		Midpoint[a]	Upper-end[b]	100% FPL[c]	Full fee[d]
Oral surgery					
D7140	Extraction, Erupted Tooth or Exposed Root (Elevation and/or Forceps Removal)	142	214	0	188
D7210	Surgical Removal of Erupted Tooth Requiring Removal of Bone and/or Sectioning of Tooth, and Including Elevation of the Mucoperlosteal Flap if Indicated	250	351	0	294
D7240	Removal of Impacted Tooth – Completely Bony	385	499	[e]	[e]

Source: GAO analysis of FAIR Health and health center data (as of January 2013).

Note: Current Dental Terminology (CDT) Codes on Dental Procedures and Nomenclature are the intellectual property of the American Dental Association (ADA) as copyright owner.

[a]Midpoint fees are the 50th percentile (percentiles indicate the percentage of reported fees that are below the stated amount; for example, 50 percent of reported fees fall below the 50th percentile).

[b]Upper-end fees are the 95th percentile.

[c]For patients with income at or below 100 percent of the federal poverty level (FPL), fees are discounted 100 percent and patients are charged a $35 copayment (plus 30 percent of outside lab fees).

[d]Full fees are those charged by the health center for patients with income above 200 percent of the FPL or for those with private coverage.

[e]Health center does not provide or bill separately for this procedure.

Table 14: Dental Fees Charged for Common Procedures in Miami, Florida (331), 2012

CDT code	Description	Local dentist fee		Health center fee	
		Midpoint[a]	Upper-end[b]	100% FPL[c]	Full fee[d]
Diagnostic					
D0120	Periodic Oral Evaluation – Established Patient	$62	$150	$20	$49
D0150	Comprehensive Oral Evaluation – New or Established Patient	85	150	30	85
D0220	Radiographs/Diagnostic Imaging: Intraoral – Periapical First Film	25	50	10	28
D0230	Radiographs/Diagnostic Imaging: Intraoral – Periapical Each Additional Film	22	50	10	24
D0274	Radiographs/Diagnostic Imaging: Bitewings – Four Films	66	140	20	62
Preventive					
D1110	Prophylaxis – Adult	95	150	35	90
D1120	Prophylaxis – Child	75	120	25	65
D1203	Topical Application of Fluoride – Child	32	60	10	35
D1204	Topical Application of Fluoride – Adult	49	85	10	36
D1351	Sealant – per Tooth	47	80	20	54
Restorative					
D2330	Resin-Based Composite – One Surface, Anterior	154	250	55	160
D2391	Resin-Based Composite – One Surface, Posterior	170	270	60	175
D2392	Resin-Based Composite – Two Surfaces, Posterior	200	320	75	225
D2393	Resin-Based Composite – Three Surfaces, Posterior	255	400	90	279
D2950	Core Buildup, Including Any Pins	250	400	100	264
Endodontics					
D3310	Endodontic Therapy, Anterior Tooth (Excluding Final Restoration)	850	1,400	400	700
D3320	Endodontic Therapy, Bicuspid Tooth (Excluding Final Restoration)	935	1,545	500	814
D3330	Endodontic Therapy, Molar (Excluding Final Restoration)	1,163	1,760	600	977
Periodontics					
D4341	Periodontal Scaling and Root Planing – Four or More Teeth per Quadrant	245	384	70	241
D4381	Localized Delivery of Antimicrobial Agents via a Controlled Release Vehicle Into Diseased Crevicular Tissue, per Tooth, by Report	60	125	[e]	[e]
D4910	Periodontal Maintenance	128	195	55	135

CDT code	Description	Local dentist fee		Health center fee	
		Midpoint[a]	Upper-end[b]	100% FPL[c]	Full fee[d]
Oral surgery					
D7140	Extraction, Erupted Tooth or Exposed Root (Elevation and/or Forceps Removal)	165	325	70	166
D7210	Surgical Removal of Erupted Tooth Requiring Removal of Bone and/or Sectioning of Tooth, and Including Elevation of the Mucoperiosteal Flap if Indicated	275	500	110	273
D7240	Removal of Impacted Tooth – Completely Bony	460	750	[e]	[e]

Source: GAO analysis of FAIR Health and health center data (as of January 2013).

Note: Current Dental Terminology (CDT) Codes on Dental Procedures and Nomenclature are the intellectual property of the American Dental Association (ADA) as copyright owner.

[a]Midpoint fees are the 50th percentile (percentiles indicate the percentage of reported fees that are below the stated amount; for example, 50 percent of reported fees fall below the 50th percentile).

[b]Upper-end fees are the 95th percentile.

[c]100 percent federal poverty level (FPL) are fees charged by the health center for patients with income at or less than 100 percent of the FPL.

[d]Full fees are those charged by the health center for patients with income above 200 percent of the FPL or for those with private coverage.

[e]Health center does not provide or bill separately for this procedure.

Table 15: Dental Fees Charged for Common Procedures in Palm Coast, Florida (321), 2012

CDT code	Description	Local dentist fee		Health center fee	
		Midpoint[a]	Upper-end[b]	100% FPL[c]	Full fee[d]
Diagnostic					
D0120	Periodic Oral Evaluation – Established Patient	$36	$49	$0	$52
D0150	Comprehensive Oral Evaluation – New or Established Patient	65	88	0	84
D0220	Radiographs/Diagnostic Imaging: Intraoral – Periapical First Film	20	28	0	26
D0230	Radiographs/Diagnostic Imaging: Intraoral – Periapical Each Additional Film	13	24	0	22
D0274	Radiographs/Diagnostic Imaging: Bitewings – Four Films	46	62	0	56
Preventive					
D1110	Prophylaxis – Adult	72	87	0	84
D1120	Prophylaxis – Child	57	65	0	60
D1203	Topical Application of Fluoride – Child	34	36	e	e
D1204	Topical Application of Fluoride – Adult	25	37	e	e
D1351	Sealant – per Tooth	45	58	0	42
Restorative					
D2330	Resin-Based Composite – One Surface, Anterior	120	175	0	130
D2391	Resin-Based Composite – One Surface, Posterior	140	191	0	152
D2392	Resin-Based Composite – Two Surfaces, Posterior	175	231	0	196
D2393	Resin-Based Composite – Three Surfaces, Posterior	195	291	0	248
D2950	Core Buildup, Including Any Pins	210	283	0	264
Endodontics					
D3310	Endodontic Therapy, Anterior Tooth (Excluding Final Restoration)	685	845	0	650
D3320	Endodontic Therapy, Bicuspid Tooth (Excluding Final Restoration)	795	990	0	768
D3330	Endodontic Therapy, Molar (Excluding Final Restoration)	940	1,200	0	988
Periodontics					
D4341	Periodontal Scaling and Root Planing – Four or More Teeth per Quadrant	183	250	0	244
D4381	Localized Delivery of Antimicrobial Agents via a Controlled Release Vehicle Into Diseased Crevicular Tissue, per Tooth, by Report	59	95	e	e
D4910	Periodontal Maintenance	100	133	0	140

CDT code	Description	Local dentist fee		Health center fee	
		Midpoint[a]	Upper-end[b]	100% FPL[c]	Full fee[d]
Oral surgery					
D7140	Extraction, Erupted Tooth or Exposed Root (Elevation and/or Forceps Removal)	135	200	0	134
D7210	Surgical Removal of Erupted Tooth Requiring Removal of Bone and/or Sectioning of Tooth, and Including Elevation of the Mucoperlosteal Flap if Indicated	219	299	0	248
D7240	Removal of Impacted Tooth – Completely Bony	436	515	[e]	[e]

Source: GAO analysis of FAIR Health and health center data (as of January 2013).

Note: Current Dental Terminology (CDT) Codes on Dental Procedures and Nomenclature are the intellectual property of the American Dental Association (ADA) as copyright owner.

[a]Midpoint fees are the 50th percentile (percentiles indicate the percentage of reported fees that are below the stated amount; for example, 50 percent of reported fees fall below the 50th percentile).

[b]Upper-end fees are the 95th percentile.

[c]For patients with income at or below 100 percent of the federal poverty level (FPL), fees are discounted 100 percent and patients are charged a $45 copayment.

[d]Full fees are those charged by the health center for patients with income above 200 percent of the FPL or for those with private coverage.

[e]Health center does not provide or bill separately for this procedure.

Table 16: Dental Fees Charged for Common Procedures in Chicago, Illinois (606), 2012

CDT code	Description	Local dentist fee		Health center fee	
		Midpoint[a]	Upper-end[b]	100% FPL[c]	Full fee[d]
Diagnostic					
D0120	Periodic Oral Evaluation – Established Patient	$49	$72	$30	$35
D0150	Comprehensive Oral Evaluation – New or Established Patient	75	114	30	50
D0220	Radiographs/Diagnostic Imaging: Intraoral – Periapical First Film	25	40	30	19
D0230	Radiographs/Diagnostic Imaging: Intraoral – Periapical Each Additional Film	20	35	30	19
D0274	Radiographs/Diagnostic Imaging: Bitewings – Four Films	60	83	30	50
Preventive					
D1110	Prophylaxis – Adult	90	120	30	72
D1120	Prophylaxis – Child	65	87	30	53
D1203	Topical Application of Fluoride – Child	35	51	30	28
D1204	Topical Application of Fluoride – Adult	30	50	30	28
D1351	Sealant – per Tooth	52	72	30	39
Restorative					
D2330	Resin-Based Composite – One Surface, Anterior	150	225	30	99
D2391	Resin-Based Composite – One Surface, Posterior	160	235	30	110
D2392	Resin-Based Composite – Two Surfaces, Posterior	205	290	30	145
D2393	Resin-Based Composite – Three Surfaces, Posterior	236	350	30	175
D2950	Core Buildup, Including Any Pins	250	367	30	195
Endodontics					
D3310	Endodontic Therapy, Anterior Tooth (Excluding Final Restoration)	700	1,025	30	495
D3320	Endodontic Therapy, Bicuspid Tooth (Excluding Final Restoration)	800	1,200	30	590
D3330	Endodontic Therapy, Molar (Excluding Final Restoration)	1,000	1,500	30	710
Periodontics					
D4341	Periodontal Scaling and Root Planing – Four or More Teeth per Quadrant	222	300	30	185
D4381	Localized Delivery of Antimicrobial Agents via a Controlled Release Vehicle Into Diseased Crevicular Tissue, per Tooth, by Report	40	83	[e]	[e]
D4910	Periodontal Maintenance	131	176	30	119

CDT code	Description	Local dentist fee		Health center fee	
		Midpoint[a]	Upper-end[b]	100% FPL[c]	Full fee[d]
Oral surgery					
D7140	Extraction, Erupted Tooth or Exposed Root (Elevation and/or Forceps Removal)	150	240	30	105
D7210	Surgical Removal of Erupted Tooth Requiring Removal of Bone and/or Sectioning of Tooth, and Including Elevation of the Mucoperlosteal Flap if Indicated	260	390	30	262
D7240	Removal of Impacted Tooth – Completely Bony	500	661	[e]	[e]

Source: GAO analysis of FAIR Health and health center data (as of January 2013).

Note: Current Dental Terminology (CDT) Codes on Dental Procedures and Nomenclature are the intellectual property of the American Dental Association (ADA) as copyright owner.

[a]Midpoint fees are the 50th percentile (percentiles indicate the percentage of reported fees that are below the stated amount; for example, 50 percent of reported fees fall below the 50th percentile).

[b]Upper-end fees are the 95th percentile.

[c]Patients with income at or below 100 percent of the federal poverty level (FPL) are charged $30 per visit plus $30 per procedure.

[d]Full fees are those charged by the health center for patients with income above 200 percent of the FPL or for those with private coverage.

[e]Health center does not provide or bill separately for this procedure.

Table 17: Dental Fees Charged for Common Procedures in Champaign, Illinois (618), 2012

CDT code	Description	Local dentist fee		Health center fee	
		Midpoint[a]	Upper-end[b]	100% FPL[c]	Full fee[d]
Diagnostic					
D0120	Periodic Oral Evaluation – Established Patient	$40	$50	$20	$28
D0150	Comprehensive Oral Evaluation – New or Established Patient	77	87	40	55
D0220	Radiographs/Diagnostic Imaging: Intraoral – Periapical First Film	26	31	c	20
D0230	Radiographs/Diagnostic Imaging: Intraoral – Periapical Each Additional Film	21	26	c	16
D0274	Radiographs/Diagnostic Imaging: Bitewings – Four Films	59	70	c	43
Preventive					
D1110	Prophylaxis – Adult	78	91	c	60
D1120	Prophylaxis – Child	61	67	c	45
D1203	Topical Application of Fluoride – Child	31	38	c	27
D1204	Topical Application of Fluoride – Adult	31	39	c	28
D1351	Sealant – per Tooth	51	57	c	40
Restorative					
D2330	Resin-Based Composite – One Surface, Anterior	133	163	40	98
D2391	Resin-Based Composite – One Surface, Posterior	152	180	40	109
D2392	Resin-Based Composite – Two Surfaces, Posterior	208	235	40	141
D2393	Resin-Based Composite – Three Surfaces, Posterior	252	290	40	177
D2950	Core Buildup, Including Any Pins	271	281	40	175
Endodontics					
D3310	Endodontic Therapy, Anterior Tooth (Excluding Final Restoration)	726	795	c	517
D3320	Endodontic Therapy, Bicuspid Tooth (Excluding Final Restoration)	836	895	c	449
D3330	Endodontic Therapy, Molar (Excluding Final Restoration)	1,005	1,025	c	549
Periodontics					
D4341	Periodontal Scaling and Root Planing – Four or More Teeth per Quadrant	246	294	c	196
D4381	Localized Delivery of Antimicrobial Agents via a Controlled Release Vehicle Into Diseased Crevicular Tissue, per Tooth, by Report	69	104	e	e
D4910	Periodontal Maintenance	129	143	c	109

CDT code	Description	Local dentist fee		Health center fee	
		Midpoint[a]	Upper-end[b]	100% FPL[c]	Full fee[d]
Oral surgery					
D7140	Extraction, Erupted Tooth or Exposed Root (Elevation and/or Forceps Removal)	159	190	[c]	106
D7210	Surgical Removal of Erupted Tooth Requiring Removal of Bone and/or Sectioning of Tooth, and Including Elevation of the Mucoperlosteal Flap if Indicated	258	301	[c]	209
D7240	Removal of Impacted Tooth – Completely Bony	471	525	[e]	[e]

Source: GAO analysis of FAIR Health and health center data (as of January 2013).

Note: Current Dental Terminology (CDT) Codes on Dental Procedures and Nomenclature are the intellectual property of the American Dental Association (ADA) as copyright owner.

[a]Midpoint fees are the 50th percentile (percentiles indicate the percentage of reported fees that are below the stated amount; for example, 50 percent of reported fees fall below the 50th percentile).

[b]Upper-end fees are the 95th percentile.

[c]For patients with income at or below 100 percent of the federal poverty level (FPL), fees are per visit: $20 for a D0120 with D0220 and possibly D0230; $40 for a D0150 with D0274; $40 for a hygiene appointment, which could include D0120, D1110, D1204, D4341, and/or D4910 (if the patient is a child not on Medicaid, the visit could also include child codes with one or more sealants (D1351)); $40 for a restorative appointment, which could include one or more teeth and all of the codes under restorative and D7140 and D7210.

[d]Full fees are those charged by the health center for patients with income above 200 percent of the FPL or for those with private coverage.

[e]Health center does not provide or bill separately for this procedure.

Table 18: Dental Fees Charged for Common Procedures in Boston, Massachusetts (021), 2012

CDT code	Description	Local dentist fee		Health center fee	
		Midpoint[a]	Upper-end[b]	100% FPL[c]	Full fee[d]
Diagnostic					
D0120	Periodic Oral Evaluation – Established Patient	$49	$65	0	$55
D0150	Comprehensive Oral Evaluation – New or Established Patient	86	150	0	88
D0220	Radiographs/Diagnostic Imaging: Intraoral – Periapical First Film	30	45	0	33
D0230	Radiographs/Diagnostic Imaging: Intraoral – Periapical Each Additional Film	25	40	0	24
D0274	Radiographs/Diagnostic Imaging: Bitewings – Four Films	70	95	0	74
Preventive					
D1110	Prophylaxis – Adult	100	131	0	100
D1120	Prophylaxis – Child	78	115	0	63
D1203	Topical Application of Fluoride – Child	38	50	e	e
D1204	Topical Application of Fluoride – Adult	38	53	e	e
D1351	Sealant – per Tooth	65	92	0	51
Restorative					
D2330	Resin-Based Composite – One Surface, Anterior	160	225	0	151
D2391	Resin-Based Composite – One Surface, Posterior	179	240	0	163
D2392	Resin-Based Composite – Two Surfaces, Posterior	225	301	0	212
D2393	Resin-Based Composite – Three Surfaces, Posterior	275	370	0	267
D2950	Core Buildup, Including Any Pins	340	460	0	260
Endodontics					
D3310	Endodontic Therapy, Anterior Tooth (Excluding Final Restoration)	850	1,225	0	675
D3320	Endodontic Therapy, Bicuspid Tooth (Excluding Final Restoration)	1,050	1,325	0	785
D3330	Endodontic Therapy, Molar (Excluding Final Restoration)	1,350	1,610	0	940
Periodontics					
D4341	Periodontal Scaling and Root Planing – Four or More Teeth per Quadrant	251	345	0	234
D4381	Localized Delivery of Antimicrobial Agents via a Controlled Release Vehicle Into Diseased Crevicular Tissue, per Tooth, by Report	63	120	0	168
D4910	Periodontal Maintenance	140	184	0	128

CDT code	Description	Local dentist fee		Health center fee	
		Midpoint[a]	Upper-end[b]	100% FPL[c]	Full fee[d]
Oral surgery					
D7140	Extraction, Erupted Tooth or Exposed Root (Elevation and/or Forceps Removal)	175	237	0	157
D7210	Surgical Removal of Erupted Tooth Requiring Removal of Bone and/or Sectioning of Tooth, and Including Elevation of the Mucoperlosteal Flap if Indicated	280	386	0	258
D7240	Removal of Impacted Tooth – Completely Bony	588	795	0	460

Source: GAO analysis of FAIR Health and health center data (as of January 2013).

Note: Current Dental Terminology (CDT) Codes on Dental Procedures and Nomenclature are the intellectual property of the American Dental Association (ADA) as copyright owner.

[a]Midpoint fees are the 50th percentile (percentiles indicate the percentage of reported fees that are below the stated amount; for example, 50 percent of reported fees fall below the 50th percentile).

[b]Upper-end fees are the 95th percentile.

[c]For patients with income at or below 100 percent of the federal poverty level (FPL), fees are discounted 100 percent and patients are charged a $20 copayment.

[d]Full fees are those charged by the health center for patients with income above 200 percent of the FPL or for those with private coverage.

[e]Health center does not provide or bill separately for this procedure.

Table 19: Dental Fees Charged for Common Procedures in Pittsfield, Massachusetts (012), 2012

CDT code	Description	Local dentist fee		Health center fee	
		Midpoint[a]	Upper-end[b]	100% FPL[c]	Full fee[d]
Diagnostic					
D0120	Periodic Oral Evaluation – Established Patient	$36	$47	$0	$38
D0150	Comprehensive Oral Evaluation – New or Established Patient	68	103	0	51
D0220	Radiographs/Diagnostic Imaging: Intraoral – Periapical First Film	25	32	0	24
D0230	Radiographs/Diagnostic Imaging: Intraoral – Periapical Each Additional Film	22	30	0	20
D0274	Radiographs/Diagnostic Imaging: Bitewings – Four Films	58	76	0	54
Preventive					
D1110	Prophylaxis – Adult	80	95	0	78
D1120	Prophylaxis – Child	56	73	0	56
D1203	Topical Application of Fluoride – Child	27	39	0	31
D1204	Topical Application of Fluoride – Adult	27	30	0	31
D1351	Sealant – per Tooth	49	54	0	46
Restorative					
D2330	Resin-Based Composite – One Surface, Anterior	130	163	0	125
D2391	Resin-Based Composite – One Surface, Posterior	135	181	0	145
D2392	Resin-Based Composite – Two Surfaces, Posterior	179	242	0	190
D2393	Resin-Based Composite – Three Surfaces, Posterior	216	249	0	225
D2950	Core Buildup, Including Any Pins	265	309	0	230
Endodontics					
D3310	Endodontic Therapy, Anterior Tooth (Excluding Final Restoration)	697	995	0	625
D3320	Endodontic Therapy, Bicuspid Tooth (Excluding Final Restoration)	875	1,140	0	735
D3330	Endodontic Therapy, Molar (Excluding Final Restoration)	1,050	1,495	0	900
Periodontics					
D4341	Periodontal Scaling and Root Planing – Four or More Teeth per Quadrant	241	290	0	215
D4381	Localized Delivery of Antimicrobial Agents via a Controlled Release Vehicle Into Diseased Crevicular Tissue, per Tooth, by Report	45	87	[e]	[e]
D4910	Periodontal Maintenance	125	144	0	115

CDT code	Description	Local dentist fee		Health center fee	
		Midpoint[a]	Upper-end[b]	100% FPL[c]	Full fee[d]
Oral surgery					
D7140	Extraction, Erupted Tooth or Exposed Root (Elevation and/or Forceps Removal)	153	185	0	145
D7210	Surgical Removal of Erupted Tooth Requiring Removal of Bone and/or Sectioning of Tooth, and Including Elevation of the Mucoperlosteal Flap if Indicated	255	300	0	235
D7240	Removal of Impacted Tooth – Completely Bony	499	499	0	415

Source: GAO analysis of FAIR Health and health center data (as of January 2013).

Note: Current Dental Terminology (CDT) Codes on Dental Procedures and Nomenclature are the intellectual property of the American Dental Association (ADA) as copyright owner.

[a]Midpoint fees are the 50th percentile (percentiles indicate the percentage of reported fees that are below the stated amount; for example, 50 percent of reported fees fall below the 50th percentile).

[b]Upper-end fees are the 95th percentile.

[c]Health center offers two levels of discounted fees: 100 percent discount for patients with income below 200 percent of the federal poverty level (FPL), and 80 percent discount for patients with income at 200 percent to 400 percent of the FPL.

[d]Full fees are those charged by the health center for patients with income above 400 percent of the FPL or for those with private coverage.

[e]Health center does not provide or bill separately for this procedure.

Table 20: Dental Fees Charged for Common Procedures in Minneapolis, Minnesota (554), 2012

CDT code	Description	Local dentist fee		Health center fee	
		Midpoint[a]	Upper-end[b]	100% FPL[c]	Full fee[d]
Diagnostic					
D0120	Periodic Oral Evaluation – Established Patient	$50	$60	$0	$43
D0150	Comprehensive Oral Evaluation – New or Established Patient	77	99	0	75
D0220	Radiographs/Diagnostic Imaging: Intraoral – Periapical First Film	29	36	0	25
D0230	Radiographs/Diagnostic Imaging: Intraoral – Periapical Each Additional Film	25	34	0	21
D0274	Radiographs/Diagnostic Imaging: Bitewings – Four Films	60	69	0	56
Preventive					
D1110	Prophylaxis – Adult	92	111	0	79
D1120	Prophylaxis – Child	65	72	0	59
D1203	Topical Application of Fluoride – Child	42	48	0	32
D1204	Topical Application of Fluoride – Adult	38	48	0	32
D1351	Sealant – per Tooth	53	62	0	47
Restorative					
D2330	Resin-Based Composite – One Surface, Anterior	155	186	0	140
D2391	Resin-Based Composite – One Surface, Posterior	170	200	0	153
D2392	Resin-Based Composite – Two Surfaces, Posterior	244	290	0	200
D2393	Resin-Based Composite – Three Surfaces, Posterior	300	363	0	249
D2950	Core Buildup, Including Any Pins	275	340	0	240
Endodontics					
D3310	Endodontic Therapy, Anterior Tooth (Excluding Final Restoration)	786	911	0	643
D3320	Endodontic Therapy, Bicuspid Tooth (Excluding Final Restoration)	917	1,068	0	745
D3330	Endodontic Therapy, Molar (Excluding Final Restoration)	1,122	1,321	0	902
Periodontics					
D4341	Periodontal Scaling and Root Planing – Four or More Teeth per Quadrant	270	368	0	222
D4381	Localized Delivery of Antimicrobial Agents via a Controlled Release Vehicle Into Diseased Crevicular Tissue, per Tooth, by Report	37	60	0	91
D4910	Periodontal Maintenance	149	182	0	121

CDT code	Description	Local dentist fee		Health center fee	
		Midpoint[a]	Upper-end[b]	100% FPL[c]	Full fee[d]
Oral surgery					
D7140	Extraction, Erupted Tooth or Exposed Root (Elevation and/or Forceps Removal)	167	200	0	147
D7210	Surgical Removal of Erupted Tooth Requiring Removal of Bone and/or Sectioning of Tooth, and Including Elevation of the Mucoperlosteal Flap if Indicated	328	385	0	243
D7240	Removal of Impacted Tooth – Completely Bony	545	607	0	428

Source: GAO analysis of FAIR Health and health center data (as of January 2013).

Note: Current Dental Terminology (CDT) Codes on Dental Procedures and Nomenclature are the intellectual property of the American Dental Association (ADA) as copyright owner.

[a]Midpoint fees are the 50th percentile (percentiles indicate the percentage of reported fees that are below the stated amount; for example, 50 percent of reported fees fall below the 50th percentile).

[b]Upper-end fees are the 95th percentile.

[c]Health center offers three levels of discounted fees: 100 percent discount for patients with income at or below 100 percent of the federal poverty level (FPL), 95 percent discount for patients with income at 101 percent to 150 percent of the FPL, and 80 percent discount for patients with income at 151 percent to 200 percent of the FPL.

[d]Full fees are those charged by the health center for patients with income above 200 percent of the FPL or for those with private coverage.

Table 21: Dental Fees Charged for Common Procedures in Mankato, Minnesota (560), 2012

CDT code	Description	Local dentist fee		Health center fee	
		Midpoint[a]	Upper-end[b]	100% FPL[c]	Full fee[d]
Diagnostic					
D0120	Periodic Oral Evaluation – Established Patient	$41	$48	$0	$35
D0150	Comprehensive Oral Evaluation – New or Established Patient	63	81	0	63
D0220	Radiographs/Diagnostic Imaging: Intraoral – Periapical First Film	25	33	0	20
D0230	Radiographs/Diagnostic Imaging: Intraoral – Periapical Each Additional Film	23	27	0	20
D0274	Radiographs/Diagnostic Imaging: Bitewings – Four Films	52	62	0	48
Preventive					
D1110	Prophylaxis – Adult	76	89	0	72
D1120	Prophylaxis – Child	52	62	0	45
D1203	Topical Application of Fluoride – Child	33	40	0	31
D1204	Topical Application of Fluoride – Adult	36	40	0	31
D1351	Sealant – per Tooth	47	50	0	37
Restorative					
D2330	Resin-Based Composite – One Surface, Anterior	129	149	0	114
D2391	Resin-Based Composite – One Surface, Posterior	140	173	0	134
D2392	Resin-Based Composite – Two Surfaces, Posterior	194	243	0	166
D2393	Resin-Based Composite – Three Surfaces, Posterior	243	298	0	198
D2950	Core Buildup, Including Any Pins	217	264	0	201
Endodontics					
D3310	Endodontic Therapy, Anterior Tooth (Excluding Final Restoration)	600	787	0	499
D3320	Endodontic Therapy, Bicuspid Tooth (Excluding Final Restoration)	725	987	0	634
D3330	Endodontic Therapy, Molar (Excluding Final Restoration)	899	1,207	0	768
Periodontics					
D4341	Periodontal Scaling and Root Planing – Four or More Teeth per Quadrant	239	327	0	256
D4381	Localized Delivery of Antimicrobial Agents via a Controlled Release Vehicle Into Diseased Crevicular Tissue, per Tooth, by Report	39	48	0	64
D4910	Periodontal Maintenance	128	145	0	114

CDT code	Description	Local dentist fee		Health center fee	
		Midpoint[a]	Upper-end[b]	100% FPL[c]	Full fee[d]
Oral surgery					
D7140	Extraction, Erupted Tooth or Exposed Root (Elevation and/or Forceps Removal)	132	175	0	122
D7210	Surgical Removal of Erupted Tooth Requiring Removal of Bone and/or Sectioning of Tooth, and Including Elevation of the Mucoperlosteal Flap if Indicated	242	273	0	193
D7240	Removal of Impacted Tooth – Completely Bony	469	486	0	371

Source: GAO analysis of FAIR Health and health center data (as of January 2013).

Note: Current Dental Terminology (CDT) Codes on Dental Procedures and Nomenclature are the intellectual property of the American Dental Association (ADA) as copyright owner.

[a]Midpoint fees are the 50th percentile (percentiles indicate the percentage of reported fees that are below the stated amount; for example, 50 percent of reported fees fall below the 50th percentile).

[b]Upper-end fees are the 95th percentile.

[c]For patients with income at or below 100 percent of the federal poverty level (FPL), fees are discounted 100 percent, but these patients are charged a copayment of $25 for preventive services or $40 for restorative or major dental (nonlab services), fees are 50 percent of charges for major dental (lab services).

[d]Full fees are those charged by the health center for patients with income above 200 percent of the FPL or for those with private coverage.

Table 22: Dental Fees Charged for Common Procedures in New York, New York (100), 2012

CDT code	Description	Local dentist fee		Health center fee	
		Midpoint[a]	Upper-end[b]	100% FPL[c]	Full fee[d]
Diagnostic					
D0120	Periodic Oral Evaluation – Established Patient	$80	$152	$23	$68
D0150	Comprehensive Oral Evaluation – New or Established Patient	123	200	46	220
D0220	Radiographs/Diagnostic Imaging: Intraoral – Periapical First Film	29	50	11	36
D0230	Radiographs/Diagnostic Imaging: Intraoral – Periapical Each Additional Film	21	50	6	30
D0274	Radiographs/Diagnostic Imaging: Bitewings – Four Films	80	140	23	80
Preventive					
D1110	Prophylaxis – Adult	155	215	46	117
D1120	Prophylaxis – Child	105	160	34	85
D1203	Topical Application of Fluoride – Child	55	100	11	47
D1204	Topical Application of Fluoride – Adult	70	125	11	51
D1351	Sealant – per Tooth	90	125	34	68
Restorative					
D2330	Resin-Based Composite – One Surface, Anterior	225	400	46	198
D2391	Resin-Based Composite – One Surface, Posterior	247	375	44	229
D2392	Resin-Based Composite – Two Surfaces, Posterior	300	450	67	292
D2393	Resin-Based Composite – Three Surfaces, Posterior	350	500	85	365
D2950	Core Buildup, Including Any Pins	350	600	75	355
Endodontics					
D3310	Endodontic Therapy, Anterior Tooth (Excluding Final Restoration)	1,000	1,900	200	891
D3320	Endodontic Therapy, Bicuspid Tooth (Excluding Final Restoration)	1,150	1,950	240	1,038
D3330	Endodontic Therapy, Molar (Excluding Final Restoration)	1,400	2,200	325	1,236
Periodontics					
D4341	Periodontal Scaling and Root Planing – Four or More Teeth per Quadrant	250	420	46	320
D4381	Localized Delivery of Antimicrobial Agents via a Controlled Release Vehicle Into Diseased Crevicular Tissue, per Tooth, by Report	75	180	130	247
D4910	Periodontal Maintenance	195	295	46	179

CDT code	Description	Local dentist fee		Health center fee	
		Midpoint[a]	Upper-end[b]	100% FPL[c]	Full fee[d]
Oral surgery					
D7140	Extraction, Erupted Tooth or Exposed Root (Elevation and/or Forceps Removal)	290	600	36	229
D7210	Surgical Removal of Erupted Tooth Requiring Removal of Bone and/or Sectioning of Tooth, and Including Elevation of the Mucoperlosteal Flap if Indicated	400	750	72	357
D7240	Removal of Impacted Tooth – Completely Bony	650	1,050	240	639

Source: GAO analysis of FAIR Health and health center data (as of January 2013).

Note: Current Dental Terminology (CDT) Codes on Dental Procedures and Nomenclature are the intellectual property of the American Dental Association (ADA) as copyright owner.

[a]Midpoint fees are the 50th percentile (percentiles indicate the percentage of reported fees that are below the stated amount; for example, 50 percent of reported fees fall below the 50th percentile).

[b]Upper-end fees are the 95th percentile.

[c]100 percent federal poverty level (FPL) are fees charged by the health center for patients with income at or below 100 percent of the FPL.

[d]Full fees are those charged by the health center for patients with income above 200 percent of the FPL or for those with private coverage.

Table 23: Dental Fees Charged for Common Procedures in Elmira, New York (148), 2012

CDT code	Description	Local dentist fee		Health center fee	
		Midpoint[a]	Upper-end[b]	100% FPL[c]	Full fee[d]
Diagnostic					
D0120	Periodic Oral Evaluation – Established Patient	$40	$52	$0	$28
D0150	Comprehensive Oral Evaluation – New or Established Patient	68	106	0	48
D0220	Radiographs/Diagnostic Imaging: Intraoral – Periapical First Film	25	33	0	18
D0230	Radiographs/Diagnostic Imaging: Intraoral – Periapical Each Additional Film	14	26	0	15
D0274	Radiographs/Diagnostic Imaging: Bitewings – Four Films	57	77	0	59
Preventive					
D1110	Prophylaxis – Adult	77	95	0	69
D1120	Prophylaxis – Child	54	70	0	52
D1203	Topical Application of Fluoride – Child	30	35	0	21
D1204	Topical Application of Fluoride – Adult	30	40	0	30
D1351	Sealant – per Tooth	50	54	0	35
Restorative					
D2330	Resin-Based Composite – One Surface, Anterior	129	161	0	92
D2391	Resin-Based Composite – One Surface, Posterior	145	181	0	132
D2392	Resin-Based Composite – Two Surfaces, Posterior	179	230	0	166
D2393	Resin-Based Composite – Three Surfaces, Posterior	220	315	0	193
D2950	Core Buildup, Including Any Pins	250	350	0	125
Endodontics					
D3310	Endodontic Therapy, Anterior Tooth (Excluding Final Restoration)	650	950	0	559
D3320	Endodontic Therapy, Bicuspid Tooth (Excluding Final Restoration)	751	1,050	0	850
D3330	Endodontic Therapy, Molar (Excluding Final Restoration)	1,000	1,150	0	1,044
Periodontics					
D4341	Periodontal Scaling and Root Planing – Four or More Teeth per Quadrant	224	260	0	137
D4381	Localized Delivery of Antimicrobial Agents via a Controlled Release Vehicle Into Diseased Crevicular Tissue, per Tooth, by Report	75	81	[e]	[e]
D4910	Periodontal Maintenance	90	138	0	104

CDT code	Description	Local dentist fee		Health center fee	
		Midpoint[a]	Upper-end[b]	100% FPL[c]	Full fee[d]
Oral surgery					
D7140	Extraction, Erupted Tooth or Exposed Root (Elevation and/or Forceps Removal)	143	180	0	122
D7210	Surgical Removal of Erupted Tooth Requiring Removal of Bone and/or Sectioning of Tooth, and Including Elevation of the Mucoperlosteal Flap if Indicated	265	325	0	214
D7240	Removal of Impacted Tooth – Completely Bony	460	546	0	365

Source: GAO analysis of FAIR Health and health center data (as of January 2013).

Note: Current Dental Terminology (CDT) Codes on Dental Procedures and Nomenclature are the intellectual property of the American Dental Association (ADA) as copyright owner.

[a]Midpoint fees are the 50th percentile (percentiles indicate the percentage of reported fees that are below the stated amount; for example, 50 percent of reported fees fall below the 50th percentile).

[b]Upper-end fees are the 95th percentile.

[c]For patients with income at or below 100 percent of the federal poverty level (FPL), health center provides a 100 percent discount and charges a $10 copayment (waived at school-based health centers).

[d]Full fees are those charged by the health center for patients with income above 200 percent of the FPL or for those with private coverage.

[e]Health center does not provide or bill separately for this procedure.

Table 24: Dental Fees Charged for Common Procedures in Nashville, Tennessee (372), 2012

CDT code	Description	Local dentist fee		Health center fee	
		Midpoint[a]	Upper-end[b]	100% FPL[c]	Full fee[d]
Diagnostic					
D0120	Periodic Oral Evaluation – Established Patient	$42	$57	$0	$35
D0150	Comprehensive Oral Evaluation – New or Established Patient	74	105	0	45
D0220	Radiographs/Diagnostic Imaging: Intraoral – Periapical First Film	26	39	0	15
D0230	Radiographs/Diagnostic Imaging: Intraoral – Periapical Each Additional Film	22	35	0	12
D0274	Radiographs/Diagnostic Imaging: Bitewings – Four Films	57	75	0	34
Preventive					
D1110	Prophylaxis – Adult	76	98	0	45
D1120	Prophylaxis – Child	55	75	0	50
D1203	Topical Application of Fluoride – Child	29	40	0	21
D1204	Topical Application of Fluoride – Adult	26	41	0	20
D1351	Sealant – per Tooth	42	60	0	35
Restorative					
D2330	Resin-Based Composite – One Surface, Anterior	140	176	0	75
D2391	Resin-Based Composite – One Surface, Posterior	155	196	0	125
D2392	Resin-Based Composite – Two Surfaces, Posterior	200	287	0	150
D2393	Resin-Based Composite – Three Surfaces, Posterior	245	350	0	160
D2950	Core Buildup, Including Any Pins	242	310	0	250
Endodontics					
D3310	Endodontic Therapy, Anterior Tooth (Excluding Final Restoration)	794	1,175	0	355
D3320	Endodontic Therapy, Bicuspid Tooth (Excluding Final Restoration)	991	1,275	0	425
D3330	Endodontic Therapy, Molar (Excluding Final Restoration)	1,136	1,395	0	519
Periodontics					
D4341	Periodontal Scaling and Root Planing – Four or More Teeth per Quadrant	215	266	0	600
D4381	Localized Delivery of Antimicrobial Agents via a Controlled Release Vehicle Into Diseased Crevicular Tissue, per Tooth, by Report	37	43	[e]	[e]
D4910	Periodontal Maintenance	122	150	[e]	[e]

CDT code	Description	Local dentist fee		Health center fee	
		Midpoint[a]	Upper-end[b]	100% FPL[c]	Full fee[d]
Oral surgery					
D7140	Extraction, Erupted Tooth or Exposed Root (Elevation and/or Forceps Removal)	125	201	0	70
D7210	Surgical Removal of Erupted Tooth Requiring Removal of Bone and/or Sectioning of Tooth, and Including Elevation of the Mucoperlosteal Flap if Indicated	245	319	0	133
D7240	Removal of Impacted Tooth – Completely Bony	447	475	[e]	[e]

Source: GAO analysis of FAIR Health and health center data (as of January 2013).

Note: Current Dental Terminology (CDT) Codes on Dental Procedures and Nomenclature are the intellectual property of the American Dental Association (ADA) as copyright owner.

[a]Midpoint fees are the 50th percentile (percentiles indicate the percentage of reported fees that are below the stated amount; for example, 50 percent of reported fees fall below the 50th percentile).

[b]Upper-end fees are the 95th percentile.

[c]For patients with income at or below 100 percent of the federal poverty level (FPL), fees are discounted 100 percent and patients are charged a $25 copayment.

[d]Full fees are those charged by the health center for patients with income above 200 percent of the FPL or for those with private coverage.

[e]Health center does not provide or bill separately for this procedure.

Table 25: Dental Fees Charged for Common Procedures in Jackson, Tennessee (382), 2012

CDT code	Description	Local dentist fee		Health center fee	
		Midpoint[a]	Upper-end[b]	100% FPL[c]	Full fee[d]
Diagnostic					
D0120	Periodic Oral Evaluation – Established Patient	$33	$45	c	d
D0150	Comprehensive Oral Evaluation – New or Established Patient	53	71	c	d
D0220	Radiographs/Diagnostic Imaging: Intraoral – Periapical First Film	20	28	c	d
D0230	Radiographs/Diagnostic Imaging: Intraoral – Periapical Each Additional Film	18	25	c	d
D0274	Radiographs/Diagnostic Imaging: Bitewings – Four Films	50	62	c	d
Preventive					
D1110	Prophylaxis – Adult	59	71	c	d
D1120	Prophylaxis – Child	48	55	c	d
D1203	Topical Application of Fluoride – Child	24	30	c	d
D1204	Topical Application of Fluoride – Adult	24	30	c	d
D1351	Sealant – per Tooth	43	48	c	d
Restorative					
D2330	Resin-Based Composite – One Surface, Anterior	102	137	c	d
D2391	Resin-Based Composite – One Surface, Posterior	125	150	c	d
D2392	Resin-Based Composite – Two Surfaces, Posterior	160	191	c	d
D2393	Resin-Based Composite – Three Surfaces, Posterior	190	245	c	d
D2950	Core Buildup, Including Any Pins	175	213	c	d
Endodontics					
D3310	Endodontic Therapy, Anterior Tooth (Excluding Final Restoration)	567	700	c	d
D3320	Endodontic Therapy, Bicuspid Tooth (Excluding Final Restoration)	635	840	c	d
D3330	Endodontic Therapy, Molar (Excluding Final Restoration)	801	1,044	c	d
Periodontics					
D4341	Periodontal Scaling and Root Planing – Four or More Teeth per Quadrant	175	211	c	d
D4381	Localized Delivery of Antimicrobial Agents via a Controlled Release Vehicle Into Diseased Crevicular Tissue, per Tooth, by Report	58	Insufficient data	c	d
D4910	Periodontal Maintenance	98	127	c	d

CDT code	Description	Local dentist fee		Health center fee	
		Midpoint[a]	Upper-end[b]	100% FPL[c]	Full fee[d]
Oral surgery					
D7140	Extraction, Erupted Tooth or Exposed Root (Elevation and/or Forceps Removal)	97	138	[c]	[d]
D7210	Surgical Removal of Erupted Tooth Requiring Removal of Bone and/or Sectioning of Tooth, and Including Elevation of the Mucoperlosteal Flap if Indicated	200	250	[c]	[d]
D7240	Removal of Impacted Tooth – Completely Bony	365	425	[c]	[d]

Source: GAO analysis of FAIR Health and health center data (as of January 2013).

Note: Current Dental Terminology (CDT) Codes on Dental Procedures and Nomenclature are the intellectual property of the American Dental Association (ADA) as copyright owner.

[a]Midpoint fees are the 50th percentile (percentiles indicate the percentage of reported fees that are below the stated amount; for example, 50 percent of reported fees fall below the 50th percentile).

[b]Upper-end fees are the 95th percentile.

[c]Health center does not operate an in-house dental program, but contracts for dental care with a local dentist. Dental patients with income below 200 percent of the federal poverty level (FPL) are charged a $20 copayment and can receive up to $150 worth of dental services per year.

[d]Health center does not provide or subsidize dental care for patients with income at or above 200 percent of the FPL.

Table 26: Dental Fees Charged for Common Procedures in Dallas, Texas (752), 2012

CDT code	Description	Local dentist fee		Health center fee	
		Midpoint[a]	Upper-end[b]	100% FPL[c]	Full fee[d]
Diagnostic					
D0120	Periodic Oral Evaluation – Established Patient	$47	$61	$4.6	$46
D0150	Comprehensive Oral Evaluation – New or Established Patient	78	107	8	80
D0220	Radiographs/Diagnostic Imaging: Intraoral – Periapical First Film	23	34	2.7	27
D0230	Radiographs/Diagnostic Imaging: Intraoral – Periapical Each Additional Film	17	26	2.2	22
D0274	Radiographs/Diagnostic Imaging: Bitewings – Four Films	59	79	6	60
Preventive					
D1110	Prophylaxis – Adult	89	110	8.5	85
D1120	Prophylaxis – Child	63	78	6.4	64
D1203	Topical Application of Fluoride – Child	32	38	3.5	35
D1204	Topical Application of Fluoride – Adult	31	39	e	e
D1351	Sealant – per Tooth	50	65	5	50
Restorative					
D2330	Resin-Based Composite – One Surface, Anterior	154	220	15	150
D2391	Resin-Based Composite – One Surface, Posterior	146	218	16.7	167
D2392	Resin-Based Composite – Two Surfaces, Posterior	189	294	21.7	217
D2393	Resin-Based Composite – Three Surfaces, Posterior	261	344	26.8	268
D2950	Core Buildup, Including Any Pins	243	313	e	e
Endodontics					
D3310	Endodontic Therapy, Anterior Tooth (Excluding Final Restoration)	695	1,250	69.4	694
D3320	Endodontic Therapy, Bicuspid Tooth (Excluding Final Restoration)	815	1,327	80	800
D3330	Endodontic Therapy, Molar (Excluding Final Restoration)	1,025	1,677	60	600
Periodontics					
D4341	Periodontal Scaling and Root Planing – Four or More Teeth per Quadrant	245	301	24.1	241
D4381	Localized Delivery of Antimicrobial Agents via a Controlled Release Vehicle Into Diseased Crevicular Tissue, per Tooth, by Report	60	91	e	e
D4910	Periodontal Maintenance	130	166	e	e

CDT code	Description	Local dentist fee		Health center fee	
		Midpoint[a]	Upper-end[b]	100% FPL[c]	Full fee[d]
Oral surgery					
D7140	Extraction, Erupted Tooth or Exposed Root (Elevation and/or Forceps Removal)	152	245	15.9	159
D7210	Surgical Removal of Erupted Tooth Requiring Removal of Bone and/or Sectioning of Tooth, and Including Elevation of the Mucoperlosteal Flap if Indicated	265	355	25.7	257
D7240	Removal of Impacted Tooth – Completely Bony	463	564	[e]	[e]

Source: GAO analysis of FAIR Health and health center data (as of January 2013).

Note: Current Dental Terminology (CDT) Codes on Dental Procedures and Nomenclature are the intellectual property of the American Dental Association (ADA) as copyright owner.

[a]Midpoint fees are the 50th percentile (percentiles indicate the percentage of reported fees that are below the stated amount; for example, 50 percent of reported fees fall below the 50th percentile).

[b]Upper-end fees are the 95th percentile.

[c]For patients with income at or below 100 percent of the federal poverty level (FPL), fees are discounted 90 percent and patients are charged a $25 copayment.

[d]Full fees are those charged by the health center for patients with income above 200 percent of the FPL or for those with private coverage.

[e]Health center does not provide or bill separately for this procedure.

Table 27: Dental Fees Charged for Common Procedures in San Angelo, Texas (768), 2012

CDT code	Description	Local dentist fee		Health center fee	
		Midpoint[a]	Upper-end[b]	100% FPL[c]	Full fee[d]
Diagnostic					
D0120	Periodic Oral Evaluation – Established Patient	$38	$60	$15	$74
D0150	Comprehensive Oral Evaluation – New or Established Patient	65	91	18	90
D0220	Radiographs/Diagnostic Imaging: Intraoral – Periapical First Film	22	30	6	32
D0230	Radiographs/Diagnostic Imaging: Intraoral – Periapical Each Additional Film	18	25	6	29
D0274	Radiographs/Diagnostic Imaging: Bitewings – Four Films	51	65	14	68
Preventive					
D1110	Prophylaxis – Adult	75	96	21	105
D1120	Prophylaxis – Child	55	72	17	85
D1203	Topical Application of Fluoride – Child	30	40	8	38
D1204	Topical Application of Fluoride – Adult	25	40	8	38
D1351	Sealant – per Tooth	48	60	9	47
Restorative					
D2330	Resin-Based Composite – One Surface, Anterior	126	180	28	140
D2391	Resin-Based Composite – One Surface, Posterior	139	193	31	155
D2392	Resin-Based Composite – Two Surfaces, Posterior	180	242	40	200
D2393	Resin-Based Composite – Three Surfaces, Posterior	228	300	48	240
D2950	Core Buildup, Including Any Pins	225	300	23	113
Endodontics					
D3310	Endodontic Therapy, Anterior Tooth (Excluding Final Restoration)	645	850	490[e]	490
D3320	Endodontic Therapy, Bicuspid Tooth (Excluding Final Restoration)	715	950	580e	580
D3330	Endodontic Therapy, Molar (Excluding Final Restoration)	948	1,150	f	f
Periodontics					
D4341	Periodontal Scaling and Root Planing – Four or More Teeth per Quadrant	204	275	100[e]	100
D4381	Localized Delivery of Antimicrobial Agents via a Controlled Release Vehicle Into Diseased Crevicular Tissue, per Tooth, by Report	63	80	f	f
D4910	Periodontal Maintenance	112	158	120[e]	120

CDT code	Description	Local dentist fee		Health center fee	
		Midpoint[a]	Upper-end[b]	100% FPL[c]	Full fee[d]
Oral surgery					
D7140	Extraction, Erupted Tooth or Exposed Root (Elevation and/or Forceps Removal)	137	187	148[e]	148
D7210	Surgical Removal of Erupted Tooth Requiring Removal of Bone and/or Sectioning of Tooth, and Including Elevation of the Mucoperlosteal Flap if Indicated	227	322	257[e]	257
D7240	Removal of Impacted Tooth – Completely Bony	390	390	[f]	[f]

Source: GAO analysis of FAIR Health and health center data (as of January 2013).

Note: Current Dental Terminology (CDT) Codes on Dental Procedures and Nomenclature are the intellectual property of the American Dental Association (ADA) as copyright owner.

[a]Midpoint fees are the 50th percentile (percentiles indicate the percentage of reported fees that are below the stated amount; for example, 50 percent of reported fees fall below the 50th percentile).

[b]Upper-end fees are the 95th percentile.

[c]100 percent federal poverty level (FPL) are fees charged by the health center for patients with income at or below 100 percent of the FPL.

[d]Full fees are those charged by the health center for patients with income above 200 percent of the FPL or for those with private coverage.

[e]Health center does not discount this service.

[f]Health center does not provide or bill separately for this procedure.

Appendix V: GAO Contact and Staff Acknowledgments

GAO Contact	Katherine Iritani, (202) 512-7114, or iritanik@gao.gov
Staff Acknowledgments	In addition to the individual named above, Kim Yamane, Assistant Director; George Bogart; Carolyn Fitzgerald; Mollie Hertel; Elizabeth Morrison; and Terry Saiki made key contributions to this report.

Related GAO Products

Oral Health: Efforts Under Way to Improve Children's Access to Dental Services, but Sustained Attention Needed to Address Ongoing Concerns. GAO-11-96. Washington, D.C.: November 30, 2010.

Medicaid: State and Federal Actions Have Been Taken to Improve Children's Access to Dental Services, but More Can Be Done. GAO-10-112T. Washington, D.C.: October 7, 2009.

Medicaid: State and Federal Actions Have Been Taken to Improve Children's Access to Dental Services, but Gaps Remain. GAO-09-723. Washington, D.C.: September 30, 2009.

Medicaid: Extent of Dental Disease in Children Has Not Decreased, and Millions Are Estimated to Have Untreated Tooth Decay. GAO-08-1121. Washington, D.C.: September 23, 2008.

Health Resources and Services Administration: Many Underserved Areas Lack a Health Center Site, and the Health Center Program Needs More Oversight. GAO-08-723. Washington, D.C.: August 8, 2008.

Medicaid: Concerns Remain about Sufficiency of Data for Oversight of Children's Dental Services. GAO-07-826I. Washington, D.C.: May 2, 2007.

Oral Health: Factors Contributing to Low Use of Dental Services by Low-Income Populations. GAO/HEHS-00-149. Washington, D.C.: September 11, 2000.

Oral Health: Dental Disease Is a Chronic Problem Among Low-Income Populations. GAO/HEHS-00-72. Washington, D.C.: April 12, 2000.